Also by Willard Spiegelman

Wordsworth's Heroes

*The Didactic Muse: Scenes of Instruction
in Contemporary American Poetry*

*Majestic Indolence: English Romantic Poetry
and the Work of Art*

*How Poets See the World: The Art of Description
in Contemporary Poetry*

*Love, Amy: The Selected Letters
of Amy Clampitt* (editor)

*Imaginative Transcripts:
Selected Literary Essays*

Seven Pleasures

Seven Pleasures

Essays on
Ordinary Happiness

Willard Spiegelman

Farrar, Straus and Giroux
New York

FARRAR, STRAUS AND GIROUX
18 West 18th Street, New York 10011

Some of these essays originally appeared, in slightly different form, in *The Yale Review* ("Dancing"), *In Character* ("Walking"), and *The American Scholar* ("Swimming").

Grateful acknowledgment is made for permission to reprint excerpts from the following previously published material:

Extracts from Elizabeth Bishop's "Filling Station" reprinted with the permission of Farrar, Straus and Giroux and the estate of Elizabeth Bishop.

Typographical re-creation of John Balessari's painting *What Is Painting* reproduced with the permission of the artist.

Extract from Philip Larkin's "Church Going" reprinted with the permission of the Marvell Press.

Extract from James Merrill's "The Doodler" reprinted with the permission of Alfred A. Knopf.

Extract from Philip Larkin's "High Windows" reprinted with the permission of Faber and Faber Limited.

Library of Congress Cataloging-in-Publication Data
Spiegelman, Willard.
    Seven pleasures : essays on ordinary happiness / Willard Spiegelman. —1st ed.
        p. cm.
    ISBN-13: 978-0-374-23930-5 (hardcover : alk. paper)
    ISBN-10: 0-374-23930-4 (hardcover : alk. paper)
    1. Happiness. 2. Pleasure. 3. Solitude. I. Title.

BF575.H27S75   2009
814.6—dc22

                                                        2008045049

Designed by Cassandra J. Pappas

www.fsgbooks.com

1   3   5   7   9   10   8   6   4   2

To the memory of Laurie Colwin (1944–1992),
Anatomist of Sanguinity

And of my father, Jay Spiegelman (1916–2008),
from whom I inherited the capacity for happiness

Contents

Seven Pleasures

Introduction Being

his book has had a long gestation. It started with the fox-trot.
The fox-trot has no raison d'être. There is no reason to dance
at all except one—pleasure—and the greatest pleasure is calculated uselessness. One evening several years ago I stood on the sidelines at Manhattan's Lincoln Center, watching the dancers at the
three-week event called A Midsummer Night Swing. They were smiling; they were having fun. I took one look and realized that dancing
can make you happy. This is a book about happiness, about the
pleasurable things you can do to promote it and to increase a sense of
general well-being, of what is called sanguinity.

A second beginning came out of a tête-à-tête between two people
who knew they would never see one another again. Intimate conversations like this often take place on bar stools late at night in out-of-
the-way places. Mine occurred last year in transit. I had just sat down
in a plane and strapped on my seat belt when an attractive woman—
mid-forties, well coiffed, well dressed, well-heeled, and wearing good
jewelry—took the adjoining seat. After takeoff we exchanged ameni-
ties: "Where are you going?" "What do you do?," that kind of thing.

At a certain point I sensed the conversation turning toward an always uncomfortable topic for an adamantly secular Jewish agnostic like me, but because my pleasant seatmate did not seem a garden-variety proselytizing evangelist, I followed her lead. She asked about my "spiritual" life, a coded but clear invitation to talk religion and salvation. I told her—politely, firmly—where I stood. Then she said that she had found comfort, and more, in Christ and his Church during an especially torturous period of pain and sorrow in her life. Whether this meant death, sickness, divorce, or the dark night of the soul, she didn't say. And then she asked, "What is the most horrible thing that has ever happened to you?"

Seldom at a loss for words, I paused. Then it came: "Nothing horrible has ever happened to me."

In Yiddish we say that a remark like this deserves a *kine hora*, an apotropaic reverse curse: "no evil eye." Say that something wonderful will happen and you guarantee that it won't. Even worse, to speak with confidence, let alone ebullience, comes close to bragging, and bragging always invites disaster to strike immediately. Every culture insists that you do something—spit, throw salt over your shoulder, knock on wood—to ward off that evil eye. Pride goeth before a fall. "Nothing horrible has ever happened to me." There it is. It's now in print and lightning hasn't struck me—yet. Ordinary disappointments occur, the blues, concern for loved ones, moments of uncertainty and anxiety, but nothing serious, deep, or long-lasting.

"Suffering," said Wordsworth, "is permanent, obscure and dark, / And shares the nature of infinity." I have not endured major losses. I have enjoyed good physical health. I have not known tragedy or chronic darkness, only more modest shades of gray. Everyone has what I call the phantom vita: prizes not won, jobs applied for but not offered, unrequited love. So what? If you miss a bus, you can get on the next one. We should not overly lament life's ordinary disappointments, but we must celebrate—soberly, not giddily or smugly—its ordinary pleasures. If we are lucky, these will suffice.

An old friend once asked me a question like the one posed by my American Airlines seatmate. "Have you ever been depressed?" she wondered.

"I've been sad, I guess, but never for long. What do you mean by depression?"

"Waking up in tears every morning, unable to get out of bed."

"No, I've never been depressed." And I doubt that I have deceived myself.

Because I am by inclination and profession a literary person, I often think—as I'll be doing in these pages—in literary terms, with literary echoes in my ears or never far from my thoughts. I was reminded of Paul Ivory, a character in Shirley Hazzard's *The Transit of Venus*, who says, "I have never suffered greatly . . . If you can reach fifty without a catastrophe, you've won. You've got away with it." "Got away with it" implies you've committed a felony, that your happiness has outwitted our common fate, that you have circumvented destiny. Life has looked positively on me. I have got away with it. Luck, or perhaps more than luck, has followed me.

Four years ago I was having lunch at a businessman's pub in central London with a college classmate, a journalist married to an Irishwoman and a longtime resident of the British Isles. Well-fed bankers in their bespoke Savile Row pinstriped suits surrounded us on all sides. We had just turned sixty. "Peter," I asked, "if you were to die tomorrow, would you be able to say that you'd had a happy life?"

"Yes," he replied. "Would you?"

"Yes," I shot back, gratefully. "This is why I don't want to die tomorrow." A decade earlier, a week following my fiftieth birthday, I had sunk into a momentary, uncharacteristic mini-depression, not quite a full-blown existential crisis or the dark night of the soul, just a dreary afternoon of clouded vision. Outside, it was January, bleak, gray, cold, and wet. Inside, I asked myself what life meant. And then it came to me: I realized that when one is fifty, life is more than half over, which is not necessarily true at forty. And, therefore, after fifty, one should not do anything one does not want to do, unless it is absolutely necessary. The happy man becomes a sprightlier version of Melville's Bartleby the Scrivener. "Can you come to dinner next week?" "I'm so sorry, I won't be able to." "Will you serve on this committee to change the university calendar?" "I'm sorry, I would prefer not to." No further defense, explanation, apology required. What a relief. Pleasure begins to trump duty. Voltaire said that "the pursuit of pleasure must be the goal of every rational person," and if you add maturity to rationality as a factor to account for, then after fifty it's pleasure all the way.

I had a happy childhood. I was a dreamy kid, distant, vague, *dégagé*, and as an adolescent somewhat surly. Never violent or aggressive, I preferred sarcasm, the little nasty remark, the occasional slammed door, and the retreat to the lair of my bedroom: that was the extent of my adolescent rebellion. No Sturm und Drang. I smoked cigarettes. I never would have thought of disobeying or running away. I was a good, relatively normal, suburban boy, figuring out the facts of life with some help from my friends, and enjoying the pleasures of reading, writing, and school, the one place (as opposed to the playing fields or most other venues in the outside world) where I felt genuinely comfortable. "Safe as libraries, safe as schoolrooms" instead of "safe as houses" might have been my motto. And schoolteachers were—although not godlike—my role models. My parents weren't intellectual or cultured enough for me: that was my biggest gripe with them. Once I had left home, set out in the world, and seen something of it, I realized that I had nothing to complain about. I had it made.

Home is where safety begins, and safety leads to ease. Ease can promote happiness, or at least its illusion. Life in the 1950s, which cultural historians often label the conformist decade, had at least one thing going for it. In spite of the cultural turmoil simmering and about to erupt in political and social upheaval, protests, assassinations, and war, America was calm for one brief moment. Call it the moment of the suburbs. And we, the children of the "Greatest Generation," grew up in it. We participated in the last flowering of truly middle-class culture. The so-called sameness of the suburbs had several advantages, one of which was—from the child's perspective—the lack of something to envy. Some of my friends lived in bigger houses and their parents drove fancier cars. Some people took extended vacations. The sophisticated ones (not too many) went to Europe. Mothers, few of whom had jobs, left back doors unlocked; in my neighborhood of two blocks of thirty-six fairly identical prewar houses, kids wandered in and out as though getting ready for dorm living a decade later.

The fiftieth anniversary of the publications of *On the Road* and *Howl* in 2006–2007 reminded us of the perpetual attraction of rebellion against the norm, of protest against conformity, of lighting out for the territory on the open road. Every chapter of American history, from *Huckleberry Finn* to *Thelma and Louise*, has its version of the road trip, the impulse to break away. The fiftieth anniversary of *Peyton Place* went rather less noticed, in part because the book's literary reputation has not held up well, in part because its lurid revelations seem much tamer in the age of *Melrose Place* and *Desperate Housewives*. Most of us lead our lives between the twin poles of escape and confinement, somewhere between the urge to break free and the intolerable neural itch to engage in hanky-panky at home.

No one in my teenage set drank, let alone took drugs. Grown-ups enjoyed the social cocktail, and although some of them—we discovered when we reached college—had serious problems with alcohol, I never noticed any bad behavior. I had one friend whose parents had divorced; she lived as an only child with her mother in an apartment. We all felt an unspoken sympathy for her, although she didn't seem to feel sorry for herself. Everyone else had two parents, siblings, and a house with front and back yards. Of what might have been festering beneath the placid veneer of domestic surfaces I had, needless to say, no idea. Later, we found out that two sets of neighbors were swapping partners, and, by the late sixties, marriages began to crumble, or at least to rearrange themselves. But in the fifties we all seemed to lead a generic life.

When I was in high school our group played a parlor game: Would you rather be happy or smart? We never asked ourselves, however, why one condition should preclude the other. The tacit implication was that they did; adolescents tend to wallow in their suburban angst. We thought happiness much overrated and, even worse, mindless. "To think is to be full of sorrow / And leaden-eyed despairs," wrote Keats in the "Ode to a Nightingale." We understood that perfectly. We wanted genius. We nervously prized our self-consciousness; we liked to think. We thought a lot, mostly about ourselves and our thinking. We read Freud and we talked about sex. Talk: that's as far as most of us got, for all our bookish sophistication. In high school I was introduced to a group of good American Christian teenagers from Abilene, Texas. They went to church every Sunday morning. They spent every Saturday night in the barn doing what came naturally. At eighteen some of the girls were already pregnant and everyone was getting ready for marriage.

Such was not our lot, children of middle-class Jewish professional parents. We weren't tormented, just adolescent. We did not misbehave. My high school friend, the late novelist Laurie Colwin, that other anatomist of sanguinity, once remarked, "Show me a happy adolescent and I'll show you a psychopath." Colwin was exaggerating, of course, in her pronouncement. All writers do. People who commit foul crimes as teenagers or adults aren't or weren't normal unhappy kids but psychotic felons-in-the-making. We, by comparison, were Baby Beatniks, wearing black and scowling, pretending to be misunderstood by those bourgeois numskulls, our parents. We were, in other words, right on schedule.

Four years in college opened my eyes to people from different backgrounds, social classes, and religions. Mostly, these years deepened my adolescent habits and solidified who I had already become. We call the university our alma mater because it nourishes. Then came graduate school and, at the age of twenty-six, a geographical exile to somewhere far away, and the start of a professional life. Decades later I attended my twenty-fifth-year college reunion. It marked the first time I'd ever done anything in the Department of Organized Nostalgia. Never wanting to look back, I had little inclination to wallow in sentiment for its own sake, but I had a legitimate, modest curiosity about my several hundred classmates, many of whom put in an appearance. We had a pleasant weekend, gorgeous New England weather, and the gratifying frustration that comes from nipping conversation in the bud rather than allowing it to go on too long.

After the reunion I had lunch with a classmate. His weekend experience had differed from mine, and it had intimidated him. A fiercely independent, liberal filmmaker, he thought that our classmates were taking only the economic measure of everyone and he felt that he had come up short. But I reminded him: we had all been eighteen years old together. We saw these men, then boys, vomiting out of dorm windows, behaving badly, and making fools of themselves. Now one of them is a hedge fund manager, while another trims hedges in rural Alabama. So what? That's how life works out. These were facts, not judgments. Is the plutocrat necessarily happier or more successful than the day laborer? Of course not. "Counted sweetest / By those who ne'er succeed" (Emily Dickinson), success is the American bitch goddess and lives by inciting us to Envy, one of the seven deadly sins. We should, I reminded my pal, envy not the wealthy but the contented.

I wonder whether the medieval four humors do not offer as persuasive a way of understanding human psychology as anything more complex, Freudian, or up-to-date. Blood is for sanguinity and cheerfulness; choler for anger; black bile for melancholy; phlegm for sloth. As with the parlor game of birth order—a subject about which everyone has anecdotal and personal evidence—or with the cardinal virtues and seven deadly sins of Catholicism, which you can observe in yourself, so also with the four humors. You can rate yourself according to how and where you fit in. I'm lucky to have come from a gene pool of sanguinity, infused with a modest dose of phlegm. For happiness, as for physical well-being, a good piece of advice is to pick your parents carefully. Start with genetic predisposition. Continue with a stable home environment. Even if you don't like it too much, as long as there is enough to eat and something to occupy your interests, you'll be all right. James Boswell recounts a discussion with Samuel Johnson, a deeply melancholic man, about an unnamed "ingenious gentleman" who had "a constant firmness of mind . . . after a laborious day, and amidst a multiplicity of cares and anxieties, he would sit down with his sisters and be quite cheerful and good-humoured. Such a disposition, it was observed, was a happy gift of nature." Also blessed with cheerfulness, Dr. Johnson's slightly younger contemporary Jane Austen gives in her last novel, *Persuasion*, a memorable evaluation of a Mrs. Smith, who has fallen into reduced circumstances: "Here was that elasticity of mind, that disposition to be comforted, that power of turning readily from evil to good, and of finding employment which carried her out of herself, which was from Nature alone. It was the choicest gift of Heaven."

"Hap" means chance, and Nature's chanciest gift is happiness itself. Call it Nature, call it Grace, call it Heaven, or call it Genetic Destiny: the source counts for less than the gift. But more than a gift, happiness is also a custom, something that can be cultivated. Nurture can affect nature. Aristotle said that we are what we do, that excellence is a habit. Like excellence, justice, or any of the other Aristotelian virtues, and like elasticity of mind, happiness may come through grace or birth, but it may also come through training. It replicates itself via repetition. In *On Beauty and Being Just*, Elaine Scarry says that "beauty brings copies of itself into being," so that the observer, merely by staring and concentrating, can prolong contact with beauty and internalize it. As with beauty, so with happiness. And because our experience of beauty often disposes us to happiness, several of the following essays deal with the realm of the aesthetic: the visual and musical arts, dancing, and reading. The sanguine temperament; the nature of cheerfulness; the things that sanguinics, or at least I, do; and the things one can do to produce cheerfulness—these are the subjects of this book. We can start out happy, but we can also make ourselves happy.

Happiness—an elusive feeling, an ambiguous term—has received less respect and less serious attention than melancholy, its traditional opposite. The famous opening sentence of Tolstoy's *Anna Karenina* ("All happy families are alike; each unhappy family is unhappy in its own way") has become an epigrammatic dictum. But suppose this were—indeed, suppose it *is*—not the case? Suppose that sanguinity, the most condescended to of the four medieval humors, is not only the most enviable but also the richest, the most varied, the most complex of them all? That each happy person is happy differently? Melancholy (black bile) has had its anatomists—philosophers, scientists, and medical people—from Robert Burton, through Kierkegaard, to Freud. Choler is the stuff of most drama in life and onstage. Phlegm has become connected to indolence and torpor, to lack of energy. Like the other two dark humors, it is treatable via pharmacology. We use meditation, as well as medication and other forms of self-improvement, to snap us out of despair, to address a chemical or emotional imbalance. But no one ever seeks to correct an overabundance of cheerfulness. Instead, people simply believe that sanguinity is at best a fleeting sensation, an unattainable goal, or, more commonly, a sign of repression and denial: "Pollyanna isn't *really* happy; she simply is unaware of the depths of her despair." Depression does not necessarily cause, or its opposite diminish, soulfulness.

Unlike my airline seatmate, I have not found salvation through religion, and unlike my other, habitually depressed friend who woke up in tears, unable to get out of bed, I have not required psychopharmacology. The twin pillars of the American happiness industry have left only a small middle space for those of us whose optimism, and the means of obtaining it, are purely secular. We turn neither to religion nor to chemistry.

The American character has traditionally taken happiness as a destiny and a right. If we are unhappy, or so the thinking goes, perhaps the fault is ours. And we have the obligation and chance to remedy our bad fate. At its most banal, the need for and the pursuit of happiness have given rise to self-help books by the score, and to television gurus who put their guests through the rapid paces of a quick course in Psychology Lite. At its most distressing, the pursuit of happiness leads to the equation of satisfaction with instant gratification or wealth, or to sudden religious conversions, the joy of accepting Jesus as one's personal savior. Such is the legacy of what Harold Bloom has called the American Religion, a form of radical Protestantism that has held sway since the eighteenth century.

The quest for happiness has deep roots in at least one side of New England transcendentalism, the serious optimism of Thoreau, Emerson, and Whitman, and the largeness of spirit we associate with the American Renaissance. These are roots whose first modern fruit was the 1901–02 lectures of William James that became *Varieties of Religious Experience*, with its acknowledgment of the "religion of healthy-mindedness" as one such variety. James allows that "in many persons" (and not just "those who are animally happy"), "happiness is congenital and irreclaimable." Staking his claims in the psychology of religion and not in secular happiness, James predicted what would become in the hands of Norman Vincent Peale and other famous descendants in the twentieth century the power of positive thinking and the "mind cure" that have swept through our country since his day. Citing Whitman, James describes "a temperament organically weighted on the side of cheer and fatally forbidden to linger, as those of opposite temperament linger, over the darker aspects of the universe." Laughter, he allows, like enjoyment of any sort, conduces to a happy existence.

To many Europeans, the belief in happiness easily obtained offers the clearest proof of American naïveté, of the jejune idiocies of the New World. Graham Greene, a man who knew simple pleasures and experienced euphoria, did not take either as an inalienable right, because his generation had come of age during the First World War, which taught them that suffering was constant and hopes for happiness inane: "Point me out the happy man and I will point you out either egotism, selfishness, evil—or else an absolute ignorance." In 1846, Flaubert named in a letter the three requirements for happiness—"to be stupid, selfish, and have good health"—but then added, "If stupidity is lacking, all is lost." Like Greene, who found the American national ideal of the pursuit of happiness enshrined in the Constitution to be merely an excuse for greed, acquisitiveness, and materialism, Thomas Hardy refused an invitation to visit the States because our national policy of good cheer was antithetical to his own gloomier views. An academic friend of mine was discussing employment offers with his thesis advisor, a dour, distinguished Scotsman who, when Carl wondered whether a job at a certain university might bring him happiness, said with pity and wonder, "My dear boy, who ever said that happiness was in the cards?" Thus, the Old World when confronted with the Thoreauvian eagerness of the New. Sophocles knew the grim truth: "Count no man happy until he's dead."

It is too simple a distinction: the giddily self-obsessed American, eager for pleasure, advancement, wealth, and well-being, versus the Old World sophisticate with a tragic and communitarian philosophy tested in the fires of centuries of war, deprivation, and sorrow. The world has seen happy Europeans, melancholy Americans. Among the poets, who often know best, John Milton strikes a harmonious balance in his youthful poems "L'Allegro" and "Il Penseroso," offering two takes on human types, the cheerful and the thoughtful, the sanguine and the melancholy. In his quest for "heart-easing Mirth" and a life of "unreproved pleasures free," the Allegro personality includes love of landscape, of music and dancing, of sociability amid "the busy hum of men." His rival and opposite prefers contemplation and solitude, a "peaceful hermitage" where he can sit "Till old experience do attain / To something like prophetic strain." I'm hoping to go Milton one better and suggest a synthesis between the fun-loving, sunshine partygoer of the pair and the studious contemplative in the "cloister's pale." Ludwig Wittgenstein, that philosopher of severe demeanor and austere habits who apparently spent his happiest times in the trenches during World War I, said surprisingly on his deathbed: "Tell them I've had a wonderful life." Who would have thought it possible?

In "Resolution and Independence," his 1802 poem of vocational and existential crisis, Wordsworth recounts his fall into a depressive moment only *because* of his acknowledgment of constitutional happiness:

IV

But, as it sometimes chanceth, from the might
Of joy in minds that can no further go,
As high as we have mounted in delight
In our dejection do we sink as low;
To me that morning did it happen so;
And fears and fancies thick upon me came;
Dim sadness—and blind thoughts, I knew not, nor could name.

V

I heard the sky-lark warbling in the sky;
And I bethought me of the playful hare:
Even such a happy Child of earth am I;
Even as these blissful creatures do I fare;
Far from the world I walk, and from all care;
But there may come another day to me—
Solitude, pain of heart, distress, and poverty.

VI

My whole life I have lived in pleasant thought,
As if life's business were a summer mood;
As if all needful things would come unsought
To genial faith, still rich in genial good;
But how can He expect that others should
Build for him, sow for him, and at his call
Love him, who for himself will take no heed at all?

This "happy Child of earth," who in fact had suffered a nervous breakdown in his mid-twenties seven years before he wrote this poem, registers the dangers of consciousness itself, especially when directed to the future ("another day"). He worries about pain of heart and all the natural shocks that flesh is heir to. Self-reliance has its own perils. But the wandering poet meets a leech-gatherer, someone far worse off than he, and the living embodiment of the poem's allegorical title. This visual reminder of *real* pain snaps the anxious speaker out of his self-imposed blindness and fears. Happiness prevails. It always does—as Wordsworth acknowledges in his epic autobiography, *The Prelude*—in someone whose earliest years have given him a base from which to construct a character. Wordsworth's mother died when he was seven, and his father five years later. He had, however, built up sufficient early strength to endure the buffets and losses, the breakups and breakdowns, visited upon him.

On this side of the Great Pond, not all Americans maintain the compulsory national belief in progress, the individual's need, and a constitutionally guaranteed right to keep smiling. The novelist Jean Stafford bitingly observed, "Happy people don't need to have fun." Or take our former Poet Laureate, Louise Glück, whose work until quite recently has embodied acerbic irony and a reluctance to acknowledge ordinary contentment. She says that we "live in a culture almost fascistic in its enforcement of optimism." When it's morning in America, a depressive person like Glück sounds like a party pooper. But Glück says in another essay: "The function of an ideal is to compel, in our behavior, its approximation. Thus the fantasy of perfect goodness and craving toward it inspire individual acts of goodness (also, possibly, rebellious acts of violence, the furious objection to the impossible standard)." Can we have an ideal of happiness to which to aspire, just as we have ideals of justice, beauty, courage, and temperance?

If you think of yourself as both cheerful and intellectually sophisticated (happy *and* smart), you will certainly have a mixed response to a recent trend in psychology labeled the psychology of happiness. It's a movement, if not exactly a craze. One clinical experiment required some people to force a smile, and others a frown. Afterward, the subjects were asked questions about their moods. Those who smiled admitted to having positive thoughts, and the frowning others, negative or sad ones. Another well-known study, this of an order of nuns, demonstrates the positive effect of keeping a journal—we might call this the writing cure—and it has long been known that meditation increases gamma waves, necessary for perception, consciousness, all higher activity, in the brain. The body possesses its own intelligence, which may influence and even surpass the brain's. Anyone who regularly deals with hard-of-hearing people will recognize the truth that when you have to raise your voice, indeed holler, at—for example—your deaf parents, although you may not be angry to begin with, by the end of the conversation you are seething with something like rage. Hostility doesn't make you scream. It's the other way around: having to scream increases your irascibility. Where the body leads, the spirit will follow.

So why not try smiling and see where it takes you? "Positive" psychology sounds too good, even insipid, to be true or to be believed. Worldly academics like me maintain a suspicion of happiness so easily acquired. "When you're smiling, the whole world smiles with you": the jaunty words of the old song inspire both foot-tapping and a skeptical shudder. When I began teaching, I was nonplussed by the genuine openness of my bright-faced students. Writing an informal assignment, many described how "my mom" or "my dad" was "my best friend." I winced. Who do they think they are? Whom do they think they are kidding? I asked myself, with a combination groan and chuckle. Are they writing this way to please the teacher? Have they never even heard of Freud? Don't they know that you hate your parents when you are eighteen, and are in constant rivalry with them? But then the most shocking response came to me: suppose it's *true*? Suppose they really do have unclouded, uncomplicated, indeed extremely pleasant dealings with Mom and Dad, have grown up with Ward and June Cleaver, Jim and Margaret Anderson, parents who know best? They, even more than I, seemed to have lived in the fifties. Who brought clouds on the horizon? Who said that misery was our lot? Is this our legacy from Freud?

I believe, however, that an informed sanguinity stands a chance. With some effort, one can find contentment, happiness, call it what you will, without the consolations of religion and without the help of psychotherapy and pharmacology. In a secular age, or within a secular disposition, cheerfulness may finally win out over its sibling humors. Freud said everything boils down to love and work. In this book I don't deal with work, in the sense of vocation, or love, in the sense of Eros, reproduction, interpersonal relationships. If those things are not going well in your life, everything else may be moot. But even if love and work aren't thriving, the fox-trot might come in handy.

If it's seldom fun to be sad, it's often fun to read about or see the sadness of others. We enjoy a good cry. Part of our pleasure comes from moderate, inevitable sadism, the opposite of envy. La Rochefoucauld said: *"Dans l'adversité de nos meilleurs amis, nous trouvons toujours quelque chose qui ne nous déplaît pas"* (There's always something in the misfortune of our best friends that doesn't displease us). The misery of others increases our own feelings of well being; it fills us with Schadenfreude: "There but for the grace of God." Looking at, reading, or hearing about happiness, on the other hand, often inspires both envy and boredom. But rather than condescend to sanguinics, or treat them with ill-concealed contempt, I propose that we can trust and learn from them. It is the province of the cheerful, built into our hard-wiring, to believe that change is possible. This is one of the things that make us sanguine in the first place.

The following essays explore activities that come from and lead to ordinary happiness. I'll put it more straightforwardly: things *I* do in a quest for neither simple-minded gratification nor out-of-body ecstasy. The sanguine temperament may take to them naturally. The melancholic may take them up with resistance, but then respond to them with bodily and emotional uplift. In *The Nicomachean Ethics* Aristotle famously described the relationship between an abstraction and its human manifestations. How does one become just? By doing just deeds. Who does just deeds? The man with the sense of justice. Consider exercise. It produces endorphins; endorphins make people happy; happy people don't kill their husbands, according to Elle Woods, Reese Witherspoon's character in *Legally Blonde*. It sounds silly, but it is true. Through persistence and habit as well as luck, one can increase one's quotient of optimism, even cheerfulness.

A reader will find this book to be not quite a memoir, but not a nonmemoir either. I am in it on every page, sometimes in the first person, sometimes commenting and speculating, sometimes referring to the observations of others. The individual essays build on the assumption that parts of my life may interest others, who will find in it aspects of their own. I promise to steer clear of the formulaic advice of self-help narratives and conversion experiences. Although I describe myself, I write about activities that anyone can perform. Stendhal said: "The beautiful is a promise of happiness." For him and for others that promise is made real in the pursuit of beauty. Or, to quote another French novelist on looking at pictures: "Great painters initiate us into a knowledge and love of the external world" (Proust, on Chardin).

In "Walking," "Swimming," and "Dancing" I meditate on physical pleasures that connect body and mind. All the essays grapple with the relationship between doing and feeling, and with what Wordsworth, again, calls the "ennobling interchange / Of action from without and from within" by which we attach ourselves to the world. The sanguine person derives pleasure from the performance and the pursuit of these activities without necessarily becoming addicted to, or obsessed with, them. Enjoyment exists somewhere between choice and obligation: it initiates us into the kind of knowledge and love that Proust attributes to Chardin, that master of the everyday.

Like physical action, aesthetic attentiveness (listening and looking) and literary engagement (reading and writing) bring pleasure and confer dignity. Even writing, with which I end, has been too often depicted—as have all artistic ventures—as the province of neurosis and pain. The cases of such long-lived artists as Shaw, Goethe, and Hugo prove that (according to John Updike) "writing can be a healthy, life-giving activity, sustainable—in Shaw's case with the help of teetotalism, vegetarianism, and bicycling—through a generous mortal span." In addition, my subjects are all familiar ones. Out of ordinary routine come both the creation and the enjoyment of art, as well as the perpetuation of happiness. I approach my subjects, as Michael Kimmelman says of himself in the opening of *The Accidental Masterpiece*, in the spirit of the loving amateur, someone whose life has been enriched by art. I also take to heart Giorgio Morandi's remark that "nothing can be more abstract, more unreal, than what we actually see." Everything comes down to the mind and the body, to the relationship between our somatic, sensuous, and aesthetic apprehension of the world and our thinking about it.

This is also a book about aloneness. Everything I write about, with the exception of dancing, is best accomplished unaccompanied. "Solitude sometimes is best society," as Adam says, albeit with perilous consequences, to Eve in *Paradise Lost*. Wordsworth famously defines "the bliss of solitude." I discovered in Julia and Derek Parker's *Capricorn* that "fondness for solitude is [a] Capricornian characteristic." (Has astrology doomed me, born at the end of December?) Reading and writing, my two bookends, are usually considered solitary acts, so it gives me a start to watch young people with laptops scribbling—if that's the right word—in Starbucks and other open spaces. Reading and writing ought to be, or at least they used to be, done in total seclusion. A taste for contemplation, meditation, and being alone with one's thoughts is the primary prerequisite for swimming and walking solo, as well as for listening to music. You can talk to someone in an art museum, engaged in conversation while responding to a picture, but you cannot do so in a concert hall without interfering with the music itself.

In his early poem *Endymion* Keats asks, "Wherein lies happiness?" He proposes an answer: "In that which becks / Our ready minds to fellowship divine, / A fellowship with essence; till we shine, / Full alchemiz'd, and free of space." When we make ourselves happy, through love, or artistic activity, he says, we are magically improved and separated from mortality. We become pure light. We reach heightened, improved versions of ourselves by losing ourselves. But experiencing art whether as spectator or participant—reading, writing, listening to music, or looking at pictures—will not make you a better person. I do not make naïve claims for the moral efficacy of art or pleasure. Pleasure does not lead to ethical behavior; art does not make one a more responsible citizen. Looking at pictures enhances visual sensitivity, listening to music enhances auditory sensitivity. One becomes attentive to the objects at hand, and also to oneself. Like athletes, aesthetes can be bad people.

Elizabeth Bishop, who once called herself the unhappiest woman who ever lived, articulated a seemingly casual *ars poetica*: "What one seems to want in art, in experiencing it, is the same thing that is necessary for its creation, a self-forgetful, perfectly useless, concentration." In the same letter, to her friend Anny Bauman, she continues: "Art only flourishes in leisure time, I guess." All the activities described in this book demand some quotient of leisure as well as concentration. A sense of humor—not taking oneself too seriously—comes in handy as well. One forgets oneself in the pleasure of doing something "useless": dreaming over a book and becoming part of it; losing oneself in writing words, which, although chosen, still manage to have an independent life and their own seeming volition; focusing through the eye or the ear on the seen or the heard; living through the body in acts of walking, swimming, or dancing, in which the small ego has vanished or been transcended.

In the early years of the republic, John Adams wrote movingly to his wife: "I must study politics and war that my sons may have liberty to study mathematics and philosophy. My sons ought to study mathematics and philosophy, geography, natural history, naval architecture, navigation, commerce, and agriculture, in order to give their children a right to study painting, poetry, music, architecture, statuary, tapestry, and porcelain." Adams stands Bishop on her head. If one is lucky, one can condense and contain the work of three generations in one's own life, moving from practicality to a higher uselessness, from economy to luxury, from necessity to ornament, from work to leisure. Such a move does not betoken frivolity, or a lack of concern for worldly cares and sorrows. It acknowledges the need in everyone's life—like that of the people in Bishop's poem "Filling Station" (see chapter 3)—for a note of "certain color."

Color, like ornament, is far from extraneous. "Mere" decoration (think of "mere" in its earlier meaning as "pure" and you have a different story), like the frivolity of dancing, may constitute the necessary uselessness that Bishop demands. As we need sleep for waking, we also need color, ornament, and everything "superfluous" to help us get through life's exigencies. Pleasure and leisure offer replenishment, and replenishment increases sanguinity. Amy Clampitt, a poet whose life and work exuded ebullience and joie de vivre, said of herself in a 1982 letter: "I simply regard myself, in spite of everything, as one of the fortunate people who happen to be around." Her tone of informal contentment also contains her gratitude for her good luck—her fortune—in having been born or become such a person. It's a sense that I share with her.

In *Studies in Hysteria*, Freud wrote to a patient: "No doubt fate would find it easier than I do to relieve you of your illness. But you will be able to convince yourself that much will be gained if we succeed in transforming your hysterical misery into common unhappiness. With a mental life that has been restored to health you will be better armed against that unhappiness." Can we go Freud one better? Can we replace common unhappiness with ordinary cheerfulness, with what Wordsworth calls "a summer mood"? While acknowledging the hap, good fortune, and neurological and hormonal constitution that produce sanguinity, one must also move onward with a sense of self-confidence, with a belief in the possibility of happiness as a habit.

Life is short. On that all the authorities speak unanimously. In the

Agamemnon, Aeschylus puts into Cassandra's mouth one version of the grim truth: All of life's happiness is a shadow, and its misery, too, "is nothing, a child's rude scrawl / on a writing slate that a damp sponge wipes away" (trans. David Slavitt). And *Ecclesiastes* (3: 20): "All go unto one place; all are of the dust, and all turn to dust again." We can change the tune, but the words remain the same: Whether you think, like Kander and Ebb, that "life is a cabaret, old chum," you've got to admit that "from cradle to tomb / Isn't that long a stay," that winter will descend soon enough, that life is a series of small triumphs that ends in one large defeat, and that—therefore—we should honor the pleasure principle and the hopefulness inherent in enlightened Epicureanism. Voltaire, who had some sardonic things to say in *Candide* about unreflective optimism, also urged us to "read and dance—two amusements that will never do any harm to the world." And I agree.

1 Reading

eople say life is the thing, but I prefer reading." Thus, Logan Pearsall Smith, American Quaker aesthete, brother-in-law of both Bernard Berenson and Bertrand Russell, a Bloomsbury hanger-on, and a man after my own heart. So is the far from reclusively bookish Graham Greene, who once said, "One's life is more formed, I sometimes think, by books than by human beings; it is out of books one learns about love and pain at second hand." Reading, in other words, competes with life, parallels it, and readies us for it.

After walking and talking, reading is apparently what I did first. Arriving at the very end of World War II, I was the firstborn child, the firstborn grandchild on both sides, and the eldest great-grandchild on two of four. I was the precursor to baby boomers about to come, the surrogate child for those unmarried women at home or for the young couples who had not yet bred. No surprise: I got lots of attention.

Unlike many firstborn children, I appeared three weeks prematurely, obviously eager to get out and begin the great adventure. Walking and talking came early, at nine or ten months. And so did reading—the alphabet at eighteen months, the mouthing of legible words shortly thereafter. Neither genuinely precocious nor extraordinary, I was simply speedy. Everyone else caught up eventually, as everyone always does. My parents tell me that when we lived next door to a bakery, I, not yet two, was able to spell the word, and then say it, to their surprise.

It was a logical, although not inevitable, leap to reading as a favorite activity, the one that started earliest and has held sway the longest. I have no recollection of being taught to read, no memory of sitting on a parental lap and being shown the ABCs, no dreams of being read to at bedtime, although all these things must have happened. I like to fancy myself as a version of Athena springing full-grown from the head of Zeus: I emerged from my mother's womb ready to read. But memory plays tricks, and we recollect hazily. The medievalist Seth Lerer says, "We live not with books themselves but with our memories of books: the bits and pieces we recall, the pages we dog-ear, the lines we highlight." I remember many books, although I also know that I have forgotten many more.

What follows is an effort to recuperate the bits and pieces of what it must have been like to be a reader decades ago and to offer some evidence of the reader I subsequently became. To imagine oneself as a reader is like any other effort to write an autobiography. You are both the same person you were long ago, and also a different one. You think you remember; you know you have forgotten. What I know is that many of my significant experiences came through reading. We read in part to lose ourselves and thereby to find ourselves; from self-loss comes self-construction.

I grew up as one age was moving into the next. The immediate postwar years, right before the national mass migration to the suburbs, opened a small window back over an infinite and receding past and forward to a brave new future world. We were the last children born before the ubiquity of television. Like most of my contemporaries and anyone older—a small minority of Americans today—I can remember life with only radio, movies, and books. For the "Greatest

Generation"—the men home from combat in Europe and Asia, the women who awaited them—and their soon-to-be-born offspring, the late forties were defining moments. Life was different, and it was going to become more different still during the prosperous fifties from what it had been in the Depression and throughout the war. The automobile and the television were the tangible symbols of that difference. New cars, new housing construction, new everything burst upon the scene. Domestic production had stopped for the war effort. My family purchased its first TV, a large piece of wood encasing a very small screen, in 1951. I was six. Watching television in the early years was a difficult, largely unpleasant experience. Transmission and reception were equally bad; everything, especially when punctuated by test patterns, looked unnatural on the tiny black-and-white picture screen. People sat on straight-backed chairs and stared glassy-eyed, as if getting ready for the psychedelic sixties, at Milton Berle, Sid Caesar, and Howdy Doody.

By comparison, reading was easy. Besides, I had already formed my reading habits. My younger brothers cannot remember life before television. By first grade I had grown accustomed to being read to and then reading to myself, having moved past the B-A-K-E-R-Y stage to children's books that did not require an adult mediator. In a newspaper photo from *The Philadelphia Inquirer* in August 1950, the summer of the Korean War, I am sitting at day camp among a group of children who are being read to by a counselor. Bored, I am looking away. At five, I already knew how to read, and how to read to others. In another, more formal picture from three years later, I am sitting on a chair in our living room. I am wearing a V-neck sweater and my hair is parted, combed, and slicked down. Alert, I look straight at the camera. On my lap rests an open book. My parents probably picked the prop for its appropriateness. I must have been eager to get back to whatever I was reading.

Unlike children who grow up in a house stocked with books, I relied—first in childhood and then in adolescence—on what I was given or later bought, or what I borrowed from libraries. Our house had few books, and I don't recall anything of interest except some of my father's medical texts, richly illustrated, printed on glossy paper, and filled with undecipherable words. My mother had some novels: does anyone today remember Taylor Caldwell? And some Reader's Digest Condensed Books, which even as a child I realized were not quite the real thing. Few children have the advantage of growing up with or *in* a library; among the interesting exceptions were Virginia Woolf (née Stephen), Edith Wharton (née Jones), and C. S. Lewis, to all of whom a wise parent granted free access to books. The potential benefits of such access are probably lost even on some of the lucky kids who have it. As a teenager I envied friends who lived in houses with books. An entire wall, or several, of warm oak or mahogany shelves looked warm, comforting, nourishing. All I could think of, naïvely, was how little trouble, noise, and bickering there must be in such a house. Books did more than decorate a room. They inhabited it like people and, like pictures on the walls, they made a room—a library, a living room, an adjoining study—harmoniously inviting. W. H. Auden kept his *Oxford English Dictionary* in the dining room because that's where most of the arguments about language broke out. The books within, like the educated parents of my friends, became surrogates for the rooms, parents, and life I wanted for my own. Families with culture, not those with money, impressed me. Speaking of what he calls "the family romance," Freud suggests that all children think they are really princes in disguise who happen to be paupers. My fantasy was that the stork had delivered me to the wrong house, that I belonged not in the palace, let alone the suburbs, but in a library.

I had, however, all around me, in the air I breathed, the reverence of assimilated, largely secular mid-century Jews for learning, study, and books, if not The Book. We are supposed to be *Am Hasefer*, the people of the book: my people assumed that reading constituted the highest calling in life, even if our justifications tended more to the practical than to the spiritual, theoretical, or aesthetic. Reading led you to advancement and success; study guaranteed knowledge; and knowledge, wealth and power. I needed no encouragement: I was hooked from the start, and although my parents tried unsuccessfully to pry me from my books at the age of ten in order to get me outside into the fresh air to play games or do chores (the opposite of what they tried to do with my brothers), I remained resolutely pensive and escapist.

I was simultaneously dreamy and attached to facts, to names, dates, and events. In a famous letter to Thomas Poole (1797), Coleridge wrote about his boyhood fascination with fairy tales, and his reasons for allowing impressionable kids to read works of fantasy:

> From my early reading of Faery Tales, & Genii, &c &c—my mind had been habituated *to the Vast*—& belief. I regulated all my creeds by my conceptions not by my *sight*—even at that age. Should children be permitted to read Romances, & Relations of Giants & Magicians, and Genii?—I know all that has been said against it; but I have formed my faith in the affirmative.—I know no other way of giving the mind a love of 'the Great', & 'the Whole'. Those who have been led to the same truths step by step thro' the constant testimony of their senses, seem to me to want a sense which I possess—They contemplate nothing but *parts*—and all *parts* are necessarily little—and the Universe to them is but a mass of *little things*.

Little things have a great deal to recommend them. Any reader soon discovers on his own steam the appropriate or compelling relationship between fact and fiction, reality and dream, parts and wholes. My passion was for history. I pored over fact books and encyclopedias: somehow they contained realities both distant and irrefutable. The almanac especially, printed in multiple columns and on almost transparently thin paper, contained the mysteries of the world, a surprising hodgepodge of facts both necessary and irrelevant. Lists of things I never knew I wanted to know about marched down and across the pages. A new almanac came out each year. One could look forward to new facts.

I remembered dates. When I was eleven I memorized—for what reason I cannot recall—the names of all the U.S. presidents, their vice-presidents, their wives, their losing opponents, and the locations of their parties' conventions. The way some kids collected stamps, coins, baseball cards, or marbles, I collected facts. Was knowledge power? I couldn't tell. For me knowledge was pleasure, and it was totally useless. Like some obsessions, it was also totally harmless.

At some level every child feels that ordinary life lacks something, and that escape from reality is possible, indeed mandatory. Some kids break out through the body; others—like me—make their escape vicariously or imaginatively. The houses of friends and relatives that contained books seemed more inviting, better equipped, and calmer than mine, which was dominated by my mother's nervous energy, an explosive hysteria that kept us on the razor's edge. Later on, the nearby Quaker meetinghouses showed me how people could sit in uninterrupted silence. Earlier, reading had the same effect.

More than anything else, reading allowed the child I was to discover parallel worlds, ones that in some ways resembled mine but in more important ways did not. I don't remember children's books, not even Dr. Seuss. Shel Silverstein hadn't come along yet. From eight on, I was hooked on the Hardy Boys, Doctor Dolittle, and illustrated history books and biographies designed for young readers. In today's educational circles, the so-called experts ballyhoo the pleasures of finding images of the self in books. Teachers and theorists want to encourage, even enforce, feelings of self-esteem and validation. Women read about women; African-Americans about African-Americans; Native Americans about Native Americans. And on it goes. Everyone holds up a literary mirror, looks into it, and finds a version of him (or her) self. If reading is really a conversation, with whom do you want to be talking? Yourself, or someone else?

I didn't go to literature to find myself. My ego was well developed by the time I became a serious young reader, and I don't think I wanted to see myself reflected, except obliquely or obscurely, in the lives of characters about whom I was reading. It was otherness that gathered and excited my energies. For self-esteem I had—well—myself, and I didn't need to bolster self-confidence by finding other versions of myself. Later, in adolescence, I went to books as much for sexual information and instruction (if *Peyton Place* and *Raintree County* seem tame today, they were raunchy a half century ago) as for non-erotic pleasures.

Even before I learned about people I learned about language, which wasn't merely referential but an essential reality of its own. Reading offered the sheer thrill of words, their sounds and half-imagined meanings, as well as information about other people and their worlds. The dictionary was my friendly companion. Our elementary school class of mostly middle-class Jewish kids recited every day both the Pledge of Allegiance and the Lord's Prayer. No one seemed to object. I believe as firmly in the separation of church and state as the next secular humanist, but in retrospect I doubt that asking us to say the "Our Father" every day did us any harm. Like all verbal rituals mouthed unthinkingly, the Lord's Prayer was less a statement of belief than a mantra to signify that the school day had begun. And it had salutary effects. Something sinks in after much repetition. I remember the mystery of polysyllabic words like "trespasses" (whatever they were) and "indivisible," words that went undefined. Here were language's mysterious enticements.

In Hebrew school, two afternoons a week and Saturday mornings until my bar mitzvah, I was filled with the sounds and rhythms of an entirely unknown language. Had there been some legitimate intellectual challenge or pedagogy in my suburban synagogue I might have become a *yeshiva bocher* (an intense young scholar), or at least stayed in the game long enough to master the rudiments of a foreign language. Each of us learned by rote his Torah and Haftorah portions, and stumbled through chanting them as his passage into adulthood. Most of us had little idea of how the words worked or what they meant. No iota of syntax or vocabulary was passed on to us.

But sitting through three-hour Saturday-morning prayers, watching the old men stand and kneel, daven and keen, and admiring their knowing what to do and their apparent understanding of the mysterious letters on the right-hand side of the page, I began to follow the service. I made hesitant stabs at figuring out which Hebrew words meant which English ones. I was becoming—although I would hardly know it at the time—both a literary critic and a literary translator. Language had opened itself to me, and opened in me something that responded to the sensuous appeal of its sounds. Even today, now that my formerly rudimentary Hebrew has become even more vestigial, I get a thrill when I pass my fingers over the words and try to recite them. At the age of thirty I enrolled in a summer school elementary Greek course. We read Homer for six weeks. The same old thrill returned: those funny characters had meanings and sounds. I could make something of them! That joy has never left me, nor has it for friends who read Arabic, Russian, Asian languages written in ideograms, anything non-Roman. Our most primitive excitement in reading comes from knowing that we have mastered the arcana of marks on a page that represent sounds, words, meanings.

The poet-critic John Hollander has described a related phenomenon, but one stemming from incomprehension and mistake rather than understanding. We all have known it, and especially in retrospect we can identify it. Joy came to Hollander from a *mondegreen*, that is, a phrase that has been misheard as something it is not. The eponymous term derives from the stark refrain of the old British folk ballad "The Earl of Moray": "They have slain the Earl o' Moray, / and laid him on the green," which became for some listeners "and Lady Mondegreen." In Hollander's young ears, the Twenty-third Psalm said "Surely good Mrs. Murphy shall follow me all the days of my life." Malachy McCourt titled his memoir *A Monk Swimming* because he heard in the "Hail, Mary" *not* "Blessed art thou art amongst women" but "a monk swimming." Things we learned by rote in childhood, whether religious or secular, stimulate our earliest feelings for the magic of language, with its multiple meanings, puns, and potential mistakes. The echoes continue to haunt us for years afterward.

All language, even his native one, is potentially foreign to a child, and all words are at one time new. Reading naturally calls us away from the book at hand to a dictionary or a compliant parent: "Mom, what does 'trespass' mean?" "What's a 'divisible'?" I asked my third-grade teacher, thinking it was like a dirigible, or a room that something was *in*. A year or two later I first heard, then read, the title of Eugene O'Neill's *Mourning Becomes Electra*. Huh? It conjured up images of a pre-noon lightning storm. Words can have more than one meaning? Polysyllabic homonyms exist? Electra was a person? Who knew?

And one book carries us to another. For me the dictionary, not the Bible, was *the* Book. It contained all I needed to know. By the time I began my first tentative forays into foreign languages (French and Latin), the Larousse or Cassell's had become practically a third hand. In my mid teen years, I got the keenest satisfaction from performing feats of translation. And from translation came some inchoate literary criticism. Skipping an entire year of high school French during the summer between grades 9 and 10, and having weekly tutorials with my teacher, I read the first book that made of me a self-conscious interpreter: *Le Petit Prince*. Talking it over with my teacher, in my schoolboy French, I said—without using the words "cautionary" or "allegory," which were still several years in my future—that the book was about the different worlds of children and adults, of innocence and experience. "*Les grandes personnes sont comme ça,*" "*Les enfants doivent être très indulgents envers les grandes personnes.*" This fourteen-year-old reader found himself poised between two worlds, appreciating both, belonging to both and neither. "*On ne voit bien qu'avec le cœur, l'essentiel est invisible pour les yeux*": so says the fox, in the book's single most important sentence. Never before in my reading experience had meaning collaborated so sweetly with charm. And the very fact that I could understand almost every foreign word—with the dictionary close at hand, every word—took the simple idea of understanding to a more profound level.

Another eye-opening experience that same year came out of an assignment in English class. We were reading *Les Misérables*. We had to write a term paper (whatever that meant for a fourteen-year-old), and I chose to do mine on the sewer system of Paris. My sanitary researches took me to the Free Library of Philadelphia, the noble neoclassical building that opened in 1927 on Nineteenth Street and Vine, right off the grand Benjamin Franklin Parkway that extends from City Hall to the Philadelphia Museum of Art. Designed by Horace Trumbauer and based on the façade of the Gabriel Palaces on Paris's Place de la Concorde, the building blended imposing dignity and generous hospitality, a combination that would appeal to a bookish teenager. This, I said to myself, was the place of learning where I could locate—or partially invent—the truth. It was a heady, even intoxicating discovery to find that I could take the bus and subway from the suburbs, by myself, walk into the halls of wisdom, riffle through card catalogues and reference books that constituted the search engines of the day, and then ask for things to be delivered to my desk. All knowledge seemed to be contained somewhere in the library's capacious, inaccessible stacks. Even better, I could make a godlike demand ("Let there be a map of the sewer system") and then have it answered ("And an early map of the sewer system was presented"). The librarians themselves seemed possessed of some secret authority; they embodied, they exuded the quiet command that comes from wisdom, or at least the knowledge that you get from books.

As at the New York Public Library on Forty-second Street, at the main branch of the Free Library a helpful assistant took a request slip, inserted it into a pneumatic cylindrical tube that whisked it away, and then the asked-for materials came back. Knowledge and power never seemed more comfortably and automatically wedded together. Reading at home, and then in school, had turned me into a translator and a critic; the exhilarating combination of pleasure, ease, and power that came from just sitting in a library made me into a scholar. Knowl-

32

edge came on demand. Learning was in so many ways simpler than life. "Ask and it shall be given" became my motto. Snap your fingers, pick up a book. Unlike people, books never let you down. They always said yes.

Books were mediums of information, imaginative escape, and pleasure. Their sheer sensuousness—the effect of looking at, touching, even smelling them—explains their ongoing power now, in an age from which the book was several decades ago predicted to have disappeared. Remember the e-book? The manufacturers are still trying to sell us on it. Publishing on demand? Perhaps. Everything in the world obtainable through Google? Still not a viable opportunity. We like owning, storing, pawing as well as poring over, our books. I remember the moment in tenth-grade English class when I made a self-consciously punning bon mot. Our genial, dapper, tweedy, mustachioed teacher Albert Weston walked by as I was deeply inhaling the aroma of a newly bought book, my nose buried in the spine between its opened pages. "What are you doing?" he asked. "Mr. Weston, I like smelling books," I replied. Skeptical, uncertain, he took it from my hand, and sniffed its cover delicately. "Mr. Weston," I snapped back, not missing a beat, "you can't smell a book by its cover!"

The physical properties of books (what we academics now call their materiality) are the first things that attract children, who know how to nibble or slobber on, and bite into, them. The very language with which we talk about reading metaphorically conveys its pleasures: "I devoured it," "I lapped it up," "I took it all in," "I couldn't put it down," "I savored it page by page." "Hungry for learning," we say. Or "It consumed me," "The characters leapt from the pages," "The action made my heart beat faster." Reading may be an alternative to lived experience, but it also makes its own physical as well as imaginative demands and offers its own sensuous gratifications. Alberto Manguel, a master of writing about reading, applies the French-Canadian word *heureuseté*—somewhat different from mere enjoyment— to reading's complex pleasures. And surely part of the provocation is the sheer appearance of the book itself. Design and marketing experts know how to draw you in, and in many ways you certainly *can* tell a book by its cover, its print, its paper, its layout, and its smell. The sensuousness of reading—especially in bed, and always holding a physical object—is another easy explanation for the failure of e-books, for the unlikelihood of a paperless society. No one ever wanted to curl up on a sofa with a computer screen in his lap. Like lovers, books entice, attract, sometimes disappoint, sometimes even repel.

Books appeal by their concreteness, as does the experience of reading them. Smell them? Yes, of course. Break the spine? Write in them? With my Jewish upbringing I took quite seriously the worship of the book, although for me such worship was more metaphorical than religious. Tradition has it that anyone who drops the Torah must undergo penance—punishments vary—and since every hand-written scroll is a sacred object, woe be unto the person who befouls the word of God. In synagogue one doesn't even touch the sacred parchment: instead, one unrolls the wooden handles and approaches the text with a metal pointer (the *yad*, or hand, whose finger leads the eyes of the reader of the text). And as the Torah passes by, on its way through the congregation, one touches it with the *tzitzis* (fringes) of the prayer shawl and then brings the strings to the mouth to kiss them. The Torah bestows a blessing. You don't kiss it; it kisses you. It is no wonder that even a nonbeliever would absorb some sense of the fearsome authority of all books.

It took years for me to crack the spine of a book, and still more years to write in one. One does not sully something sacred. When I began buying my own textbooks in college, I had eventually to think of them as objects of use. I started by penciling delicate check marks in the margins. Then came underlining. I was on the slippery slope to perdition. Marginalia followed. Little did I know that commentary—biblical, talmudic—had a long history, one sage literally layering his interpretation upon those of his precursors, as in a variorum edition or a modern hypertext that allows you to see a page surrounded by commentary. The relationship between primary and secondary, call and response, gospel truth and human ideas, began to blur. At their best, in the marginalia of great writers (Blake, Keats, and Coleridge leap to mind) we follow an author's own engagement through his response to what he's reading. He's illuminating not only a putative subject but, more important, himself. Coleridge's voluminous marginalia, thousands of pages in six thick volumes, show us a deep mind busy at work. Blake's are often more fun, ranging from grunts of commendation or disapproval ("No," "Bravo," "Sweet," "I do not believe it," "Trifling Nonsense"), through questions, aphorisms ("Noble . . . But Mark . . . Active Evil is better than Passive Good"; "There is no such thing as Natural Piety Because The Natural Man is at Enmity with God"), to whole paragraphs that reproduce in miniature the eccentric genius's distinctive worldview.

At their most embarrassing, marginalia give evidence of youth's follies, pretensions, and idiocies. In the opening pages of *Pnin*, Nabokov scores a point when thinking of the textbooks of the returning Waindell University students, those eager beavers who write things like "description of nature" and "irony" in the margins and translate difficult words like *oiseaux* in case they won't remember them in the future. I once borrowed a copy of Lawrence's *Sons and Lovers* from a colleague whose narcissism practically leapt from the page in which he'd written, in response to an excessively maudlin and mystic Lawrentian effusion on the subject of masculinity, "This doesn't apply to me." For whom, I wondered, was this written? Himself? His friends and family, heirs and students? Someone else is bound to see this. As you read and as you scribble, so you too will be overheard, witnessed, and read. Talk back to the text at your own peril. Your puerile, infantile remarks will come back to haunt you.

"Some books are to be tasted, others to be swallowed, and some few to be chewed and digested." Thus, Francis Bacon's famous epigram of what was a standard Renaissance image, one articulated by Queen Elizabeth herself. As readers, we take it all in, at the same time being consumed by the experience. Reading is a complex interchange between action and passivity. To consume is to burn, to devour. I absorbed books; they set me on fire. I savored. In the Old Testament, the prophet Ezekiel (c. 593 BCE) is visited by an angel who says to him, "Son of Man, eat this roll." In some medieval Jewish schools, boys covered their slates with words, and then with honey. They licked the honey off. Sometimes biblical verses were written on cakes, or on hard-boiled eggs. First you read, then you eat. Reading nourishes the body as well as the spirit.

Reading Ezekiel for the first time, I had one of those wonderful experiences of misreading (what Harold Bloom calls misprision, a mistake that reveals a deeper sense of truth). The roll in question was not, as my adolescent self thought, a croissant or a brioche but a written scroll, to be absorbed orally and taken into the body. To be taken to heart by being digested. One should read ravenously, as one eats. Especially to the young and the passionate, even the potentially passionate, books are erotic objects as well as vessels of eroticism. Whenever a diligent dutiful student asks me for reading recommendations, suggestions for summer self-improvement, I demur. Certainly not, I say. You must read as you live: promiscuously. You must go, as I did for years, to the local libraries and scan the shelves, pulling things out randomly, thumbing the pages, reading the openings, and allowing your eyes to wander where they will. Take shopping bags, backpacks, with you. Fill them up. Bring them home. Some things will command your attention for more than a minute; those that don't, take back. Reading must be violently fickle, experimental, capricious, and even dangerous. Find what suits and stick with it. Read only what you want. Books will not necessarily make you a better person. Instruction is for the classroom; summers are for pleasure. In *Reading Like a Writer*, Francine Prose gives us in a final chapter her list of "Books to Be Read Immediately." At best her list is an interesting aside: it shows us one woman's tastes. If you are interested in Francine Prose, then you learn something about her from it. You will learn nothing about anyone or anything else. All readers have their list of Desert Island Books, and choices overlap, but everyone must make her own and not depend on someone else's.

In high school, my friends and I were obsessed with, in ascending order, politics, music, and books. In the innocent days before the full flowering of the 1960s, the days of Camelot before November 22, 1963, before Vietnam, before the conflagrations in our cities and around the globe, political protest had an enviably innocent hopefulness that soured soon after. Everything seemed possible. The musical taste of the age occupied an equivalent middle ground, between early Elvis and the Beatles' first LP. For us, music meant folk songs, Joan Baez, Pete Seeger, the young Odetta, and the even younger Ray Charles. It also meant our first forays into classical music both on records and in performance.

But it was books above all that defined us Baby Beatniks. The new millennium promotes many ways of being or appearing smart. Today's young people boast a visual sophistication acquired from movies, television, and the assaults of the commercial marketplace. We lacked the assaults and therefore the sophistication. The media did not direct us, let alone define us. To be smart, fifty years ago, meant to read; sophistication meant, *tout court*, literary sophistication. Foreign language instruction, by now a thing of the past in most public school systems, was in full flower, in part because of Sputnik and our presumed need to compete on scientific and other terms with the evil empire of the Soviet Union, in part as a legacy of the great immigration to the United States from the end of the nineteenth century through World War II. In the thirties, virtually every small-town American high school offered instruction in Latin, German, French, and Spanish; in the post-Sputnik 1950s, Russian was added to most big city and suburban school curricula. Those days are long gone. Only the rare or rich public school nowadays offers more than a perfunctory year or two of Latin, or any modern language other than the inarguably useful Spanish.

Utility was the last thing that any of us cared about. A strong sense of snobbism operated. The smartest or most competitive kids took Latin, on the dubious grounds that it would be useful, according to our parents, in preparing us for careers in medicine and law. It had something to do with understanding the roots of English words and being able to identify quickly *habeas corpus*, *mens rea*, *lex talionis*, *stare decisis*, *res judicata*, and a host of pharmaceutical terms. The arty crowd, mostly girls, took French, the language of charm and poise. Especially after the country caught sight of Jacqueline Kennedy and fell in love with her, enrollments in French classes soared. Everyone else took Spanish, thinking it easier than the others. Sure, it lacked the declensions of Latin and German, but its nuances and pronunciation, not to mention the subjunctive mood, didn't really make it easier to acquire. But Latin was for the cream of the crop. Later, in college, some of my friends tried to outdo one another by finding the most obscure languages to study–Turkish, Korean, Swahili, even Amharic. In his autobiography *My Early Life*, that notoriously bad student Winston Churchill has this to say: "By being so long in the lowest form, I gained an immense advantage over the cleverer boys. I got into my bones the essential structure of the basic British sentence, which is a noble thing. Naturally I am in favor of teaching boys English, and then I would allow the clever ones to learn Latin as an honor, and Greek as a treat."

Latin was the honor, and as it turned out, under the guidance of an inspiring teacher and with a great book in front of us (the *Aeneid*), it was also the treat. By twelfth grade, our less gifted, less linguistically inclined peers having dropped from the rolls, the happy few still standing read and battled our way through the standard parts of the epic: Book 1 (the arrival at Carthage), Book 2 (the last night of Troy), Book 4 (the love affair between Dido and Aeneas), and Book 6 (the descent to the Underworld; Aeneas's vision of Rome's future). Other Virgilian bits and pieces, and small snippets of Ovid, also entered the picture. The study of Latin accomplished something that my studies in English and French had failed to do: it made me aware of how poetry actually works. My native language did not have the same effect on me; because I understood it, I mistakenly thought that I could read it less carefully. In Latin class we worked our way from sentence to sentence, through clause within clause, part within part; we attended to every piece of every word. Our labors made demands that English never did. We took from our teacher the first commandment: "Always Go for the Verb." Even French was less challenging, because we spent so much of our time learning to pronounce it. Thank goodness for the uselessness of the so-called dead languages.

I can barely imagine how many hours I must have spent lying on my bed or sitting at my desk, dictionary in hand, parsing the sentences. We did not resort in those days to trots or ponies (words that my students today do not know); by and large, we were fiercely proud of our desire to master the language, although the telephone came in handy for late-night consultations. When Aeneas encourages his depleted band of war-weary companions, *"O socii . . . forsan et haec olim meminisse iuvabit,"* the simple act of translating the famous speech made of me not only a translator but also a close reader of poetry. The hero was addressing *us*, his adolescent audience: "O comrades . . . Someday, perhaps even these things will be a pleasure to recall." Indeed, they have been, to me and my own companions (like Aeneas's *socii*), some of whom went on to study classics in university, and all of whom—whether they became academics, doctors, lawyers, business people, architects, psychotherapists—can now attest, well after middle age, to the far from vocational or useful effects of our classical studies. Latin class helped steer me into a lifetime of reading poems. Robert Frost first heard what he called "the speaking voice" in poetry when he was a high school student in Lawrence, Massachusetts, reading the expected plays of Shakespeare and the unexpected *Eclogues* of Virgil. He made his discovery through a poet two millennia removed, who wrote in a so-called dead language, and in the pastoral mode, that most artificial of poetic genres. His experience would have struck me as more surprising than it did had something similar not happened to me, although in my case it was the *Aeneid* that effected the revelation.

Several years before, about the time of *Le Petit Prince* and *Les Mis-érables*, big, long novels were my avenue of escape, my extracurricular pastime. When I was fourteen, *Gone With the Wind*, the first movie I'd ever seen in a big-screen rerun, years before old movies appeared on TV, came to local theaters. The film has a classic symmetry. Part 1 ends with Scarlett's vow, "As God is my witness, I'm never going to be hungry again," a condensed version of the novel's oath "As God is my witness, as God is my witness, the Yankees aren't going to lick me. I'm going to live through this, and when it's over, I'm never going to be hungry again. No, nor any of my folks. If I have to steal or kill—as God is my witness, I'm never going to be hungry again." I never knew that a movie could have an intermission. I'd never seen one that did. So I thought the film had just ended, and I was about to leave the theater. Vivien Leigh's courageous determination had left me satisfied. There was more? A chum brought me back in for the second half.

Then I read the novel, and could not, as the saying goes, put it down. Quite literally: when I got to page 1,037, I went back to the beginning and read it again. Mitchell may have seen the world of the Old South with a blinkered view, and we now look askance at her ideology and magnolia-scented nostalgia, but she sure knew how to write an opening sentence: "Scarlett O'Hara was not beautiful, but men seldom realized it when caught by her charm as the Tarleton twins were." I was hooked, and like the twins, I fell in love with Scarlett and practically everyone else in the book. Never mind that, even then, I knew that Mitchell's view of the South—with its plantation slaves as caricatures of happy, devoted, singing darkies—was inaccurate, offensive, and politically incorrect, although no one would have used that term in 1958. What held me was the book's narrative pacing, its structure, and—from the first sentence above—its language. Throughout, Mitchell's style combines clarity of diction and opulence of detail, a kind of Southern overripeness when necessary. As much as for the story, I read for style, even then. (Later I was impressed by the dicta of Chateaubriand: "We live only by means of style," and the witty Howard Nemerov: "The point of style is character.") Even compared to the long movie, the sprawling novel seemed ample and rich, the kind of thing in which a young reader could lose himself. Scarlett's vow, above, comes not halfway but one-third through, on page 428. Victor Fleming had taken Mitchell's loose and baggy monster, and tailored it for a different medium. He had given it a shape it possessed implicitly.

So I realized that form, like language, was important. In college I read E. M. Forster's 1949 speech "Art for Art's Sake," whose title represented at the time an unfashionable belief. (How could it not in the wake of World War II?) My early pleasure in the symmetry of novels made me sympathetic to Forster's clearly articulated aestheticism: "A work of art—whatever else it may be—is a self-contained entity, with a life of its own imposed on it by its creator. It has internal order. It may have external form. That is how we recognize it." As a teenager I had begun to sense the internal harmony of books, from which much of their pleasure derived.

The year after *Gone With the Wind* I found Betty Smith's *A Tree Grows in Brooklyn*. Perhaps it found me. The novel first appeared in 1943, one year before I did. It is a book about reading and dreaming, about the way young Francie Nolan gets herself out of a Brooklyn tenement through a program composed of equal parts grit and literary imagination. At the end of the book, as she leaves Brooklyn, she packs up her sparse library, which includes—in addition to scrapbooks she has assembled—the Gideon Bible, a complete Shakespeare, and a tattered *Leaves of Grass*. Francie's mother is a janitor, her father a singing waiter. Francie is a reader, going to the library, reading a book a day in alphabetical order. On Saturday she rests and luxuriates, sitting on the fire escape by the tree. After the death of her father from drink, after she leaves grade school and gets a factory job, later advancing to the position of a "reader" to the other workers, after she passes a college entrance exam and prepares to go to the University of Michigan, she turns in her library books for the last time. She sees another girl, book in hand, sitting on the fire escape. Her old tree, cut down, has grown another shoot from its stump.

From the start, I was enthralled. Two things got to me. The first had something to do with language itself. Here is the opening paragraph:

> Serene was a word you could put to Brooklyn, New York. Especially in the summer of 1912. Somber, as a word, was better. But it did not apply to Williamsburg, Brooklyn. Prairie was lovely and Shenandoah had a beautiful sound, but you couldn't fit those words into Brooklyn. Serene was the only word for it; especially on a Saturday afternoon in summer.

The words, the voice, I realized, belonged both to the author and to her main character, both of whom grappled with questions of language. What word best describes a summer afternoon in Brooklyn? (Shakespeare asks, "Shall I compare thee to a summer's day?") That's a problem for a writer, and also for a reader, alert to the ways in which language meets, matches, and defines the world around her. I was also struck by what I thought was a mistake: we had been taught even in seventh grade that "serene," "somber," and "prairie" ought by rights to have quotation marks around them to signal their presence as things, as labels. Betty Smith was doing something that would get a red pencil mark from my teacher. Maybe writers had options? Was this what I later learned was called poetic license? Whatever it was, it felt daring. It was style.

Equally exciting was the sense—the same I had when reading St.-Exupéry—that something could stand for, represent, something else. I didn't yet have a word for this. Several years later, in school, we would be taught terms like "symbol," "metaphor," the basic building blocks of literary study. The tree that grew in Brooklyn is the ailanthus, the "Tree of Heaven," a sturdy, unattractive, tenacious plant that takes root in the most uncongenial terrain. It's Francie herself; I realized that pretty quickly, especially because Smith gives us a reader's guide in the form of an italicized epigraph across from the title page:

> There's a tree that grows in Brooklyn. Some people call it the Tree of Heaven. No matter where its seed falls, it makes a tree which struggles to reach the sky. It grows in boarded-up lots and out of neglected rubbish heaps. It grows up out of cellar gratings. It is the only tree that grows out of cement. It grows lushly . . . survives without sun, water, and seemingly without earth. It would be considered beautiful except that there are too many of it.

I lived in a lush suburb, with yards and gardens and two cars in every driveway. How—what word could I think of?—how exotic, how romantic it must be to live in a slum, to escape via a fire escape. That's where life was livelier and more intense. And, if daydreaming Francie could get away from her slum, then perhaps her daydreaming male reader could vicariously transcend suburban dreariness.

Language, characterization, metaphor, formal structure, and repetition: I knew exactly what gave satisfaction even if I couldn't say so in words. A child reads first for words and pictures, then for sound and story, then for characterization. As the child grows, other, subtler factors come into play. He begins to appreciate literary shape. Meyer Levin's *Compulsion* (1956) told the gripping story of Leopold and Loeb in two parts, "The Crime of the Century" and "The Trial of the Century." Before and after, cause and effect: what clarity. Stories had architecture! Then there was Edwin O'Connor's 1956 *The Last Hurrah.* I must have seen Spencer Tracy in the 1958 movie and then turned back to the original, as I had done with *Gone With the Wind.* All the ads and reviews said that Frank Skeffington really *was* Boston's notorious James Michael Curley, but the town stayed anonymous. Something could be fiction and reality at the same time.

The floodgates opened: early Truman Capote and Carson Mc-Cullers, Southern Gothic hothouse flowers, both an escape from a perfectly ordinary Northern suburban life. So was Isak Dinesen. I moved from fiction to nonfiction: history, philosophy (somewhere I have notes from my teenage reading of Kierkegaard). Freud's *The Psychopathology of Everyday Life* looked inviting but quickly bored this sixteen-year-old. Reading became something of a competitive sport between me and my friends. We vied not only for quantity but also for speed and variety. Who could read the most outré stuff? Japanese haiku? *No Exit*? No problem. Dylan Thomas? Kierkegaard? Dante? Hermann Hesse? We knew that *The Waste Land* was important poetry although, or because, we couldn't understand a word of it. The exotic quickly became domesticated in our intense game of academic one-upmanship.

Even before we began haunting the bookstores and coffeehouses—and pretending to be sophisticated college students, not that we fooled anyone but ourselves—near the University of Pennsylvania campus, we hung out at Leary's bookstore on South Ninth Street in Center City Philadelphia, an ancient, narrow, multistoried smaller building sandwiched between the two large commercial caverns that constituted Gimbel's department store. It was a heavenly dusty haven, heavenly *because* dusty. Most big cities had such places; now they have all but vanished from everywhere, victims of the chains and the Internet. Leary's went in the mid-sixties. It stocked new books, especially college texts, their bread-and-butter business, but that's not why you went there. The best stuff was secondhand, and everything was old, the staff as well as the materials. The place was drab; it smelled. Whatever the spanking clean suburbs were, this was the exact opposite. It was no place like home, but it's where I wanted to live. Books—used, dog-eared, sometimes broken and yellowed—were the inhabitants, and they never had to behave properly. No demands were made of them.

Or of you: no one smiled and greeted you. If you wanted help, you asked. There are worse things, for a reader and a shopper, than being ignored. Better than finding what you were looking for, you found what you weren't looking for. You didn't even know what you were looking for until you had found it. For any shopper, nothing beats the thrill of serendipity. Wandering from floor to floor, category to category, you'd pull something from a shelf and find something right behind it. Accumulated piles tottered on the floor. Leary's arranged their books cavalierly at best; all order—a generous term—had a large quotient of randomness. When you made a purchase, you put your money (no credit cards yet) into a basket, which was attached to a rickety overhead cable transit system. Even a half century ago we knew this was an antique, part of the store's deliberate resistance to the fads of modernity like cash registers. The clanking cable shuffled the basket off to the unseen cashier's office; a few minutes later the receipt and change clanked their way back to you. You could stay all day. Some of the staff looked as though they had stayed forever. No one asked what you were doing, because no one really cared. They hoped you would buy, if not today then tomorrow. They knew you were a reader. Otherwise you wouldn't have come in. James Billington says he thinks he became the Librarian of Congress because when he was a kid his father kept bringing home used books from Leary's. The store was a bookworm's image of eternity.

Even more than bookstores, books themselves beckoned; they were the places we inhabited, and gradually they came to inhabit us. The greatest readers have always resorted to physical language when describing the pleasures—and pains—of this most solitary and contemplative act. Keats wrote in a letter that when we read a long poem we are liberated, by which he meant that it also captures us. I've already mentioned the metaphors of feeding, eating, nourishment. Images of travel are almost equally popular, from Emily Dickinson's "There is no frigate like a book / To take us lands away," to Keats's greater "On First Looking into Chapman's Homer," which enlivens and enriches the motif of reading as vicarious travel. At secondhand, the twenty-year-old speaker-listener-reader-writer says, he's "heard of one wide expanse" where Homer ruled, but he's never had the thrill of visiting it till he heard "Chapman speak out loud and bold," at which point he felt as though he were actually there, "breath[ing] its pure serene" air. Only the language of the senses can convey the powerful effect of Chapman's Elizabethan translation.

In the following century, Kafka wrote to Oskar Pollak about an equivalent power, but one more dangerous, potentially deadly: "I think we ought to read only books that bite and sting us. If the book we are reading doesn't shake us awake like a blow in the skull, why bother reading it in the first place? . . . What we need are books that hit us like a most painful misfortune . . . a book must be the axe for the frozen sea within us." The book destroys; the book gives life. For Keats, reading enhances and enlarges, expanding a horizon; it lets us breathe purer air; it gives a high. For Kafka, it also banishes us, it terrifies, it inundates. Kafka was not interested in soothing one's ego, in confirming oneself, or in self-esteem, at least not the self-promoting kind that comes when you are reading about yourself.

These physical metaphors come naturally from writers for whom literature is a matter of life and death, Eros and Thanatos. For ordinary, temperate readers, pleasure not pain predominates. Either way the sheer physical conditions of the act bear noticing. Like all the activities discussed in these pages (with the exception of dancing), reading demands not only leisure and discipline but also tranquillity and solitude. History changed when people began reading silently, privately, instead of aloud and in groups. In medieval monasteries, the group prevailed, communal reading took place at meals, and according to Manguel, "solitude and privacy were considered punishments." Throughout the nineteenth century, when it was difficult and socially unapproved to be a scholarly, i.e., independent, woman in Britain, ladies read aloud to one another as a socially sanctioned way of studying. The life of the individual repeats that of the species: every child reaches a point at which he replaces the evening activity of being read to by a parent, first by a back-and-forth antiphonal reading, and then by reading silently to himself. No parent need apply, no audience is necessary. The social performance has changed into a solitary event. Lost in the imaginary world of the book, the child is lost within himself, both performer and audience in one.

Later in life, reading aloud may return. Like gardening, it's the hobby of the middle-aged. I think of such famous reading couples as William and Dorothy Wordsworth, Leonard and Virginia Woolf, or the American poets Donald Hall and his wife, Jane Kenyon, and Amy Clampitt and her husband, Harold Korn. Jane Austen's family at the Steventon Rectory in Hampshire read aloud to each other throughout the day. Robert Frost said that the ear, not the eye, is the best reader. He was thinking of how the silent reading of poetry tends to elide not only words but also sounds, rhythms, all the musical qualities that go into the full sensuousness of the experience of the text. And whether silent or spoken, the best reading is always slow—this is really what Frost was talking about.

When still in high school, I enrolled with some classmates in a "speed-reading" course, the silliness of which was apparent to me even at the time. A woman named Evelyn Wood had invented, perfected, or fabricated a technique called "Reading Dynamics" that involved waving your hand simultaneously across and down the page in front of you. As if saying "abracadabra" with your wave, you somehow got the essential meaning to rise from the page and into your consciousness through mystical osmosis. It was like waking the dead or invoking absent spirits at a séance. And it was totally without pleasure. Thomas De Quincey distinguished between the literature of knowledge and that of power: the first is what you go to for information, the second for transport. I suppose that time-saving measures like speed-reading might be useful to anyone engaged in the practicalities of information hunting and gathering, but no authentic reader wants to move quickly. Readers are tortoises, not hares.

Most of us prefer marching at our individual pace. Everyone has mixed feelings about Books on Tape, a double-edged experience that allows us to become children again. The listener, in a car, at the gym with a headset, or lying on a comfortable chair beside an amplifier, hears a professional reading in a good voice, articulating with poise, nuance, passion, and intelligence, and—above all—clarity, words that might have slipped under the radar of consciousness as the human eye moves across and down a page, sometimes losing its track. But the listening reader is entirely passive, the victim as well as the beneficiary of choices made for him by another reader. It's like the difference between watching a live performance—opera, baseball, ballet—and directing your glance where *you* want it to go, and watching the same thing on a screen. You get the replays and the close-ups, but someone else has made all the directorial choices. And it also resembles the phenomenon of the public reading by Famous Writers A and B: one might read beautifully and the other mutter into his beard. A wonderful performance may send you to the book from which the reader recited, only to decide that you prefer your own version of the music to the author's.

Serious readers are solitaries for whom art is an intensely private matter. They tend to be odd, silent, obsessed, and independent or positively ornery, seldom in step with everyone else. And why would anyone want to join a book club, read the same thing as everyone else on the block, and then sit around in a circle and exchange pleasantries? Give me liberty, please. I, for one, like to read while eating (Pliny the Younger liked to be read *to* at meals, like those Cistercian monks later); one of the great pleasures of solitary traveling is unembarrassed reading in restaurants.

Some readers require certain kinds of furniture and sources of light. We were taught at school always to read in a comfortable chair that allowed for easy but not too easy posture, with a strong reading light or other source of illumination coming over the left shoulder. Marguerite Duras said she never read outdoors, preferring darkness, with only the page illuminated. I care less about posture and light source than extraneous noise. I can no longer read anything serious if music is playing. When traveling, or waiting in train stations and airports, trapped in any public space, I want earplugs to block out both human conversation and extraneous noises. I can write with music playing, because writing means pushing something out, whereas reading means taking something in. I can take in only one thing at a time, and if I choose to read, I'm using my eyes and my metaphorical ears. Anything external and superfluous will distract. Most people prefer reading in bed, and many like the prone position best. Is this a regression to childhood and the Land of Counterpane? Anyone who has stayed up after lights-out at home or summer camp with a flashlight under the covers knows the furtive thrill of both solitude and disobedience. And how many people fall asleep while reading, rather than get kicked into consciousness by it? Is reading stimulating or soporific?

In adulthood, what should—what does—one read? No longer having the luxury of youthful promiscuity, knowing that the clock ticks, that every choice of something eliminates something else, what should you do? Readers are gamblers. Every recommendation from enthusiastic friends comes at a risk. You might begin a new work and get tired, not finding its rewards and pleasures soon enough. What to do next? Stick with it and hope that the payoff will soon roll in? Or cut your losses and move on to something else? My suggestion: Reread those books that gave pleasure in the past. A photographic memory is not necessarily a blessing; there's a charm in forgetting, so if you're not cursed with perfect recall, you'll have the joy of discovering some things as though for the first time, while others will hit you with the refreshing rush of repetition. As an older version of the person you've always been, you can have things two ways at once: something old, something new; something recalled, something revealed.

When I was an adolescent, my idea of heaven involved being locked in a darkened room and reading fiction for twelve hours a day. Now I realize that the great novels are to some extent wasted on the young. When I was twenty, I read *The Portrait of a Lady* in a college seminar on Henry James. I managed to perform the maneuvers and honor the protocols that sophisticated English majors were taught, but I really had not the slightest notion of what Isabel Archer was about. I analyzed but did not understand her. James's heroine might have been a creature from another planet or a different species. Ten years later, the book made more sense. I, not it, had changed. *Anna*

Karenina—rather, my reading of it—underwent an equivalent metamorphosis. At twenty-one I asked myself, "Where is the style?" and "Why is there so much agriculture?" Mark Twain used to say that when he was a child his father seemed to him a fool, but when he reached his own maturity his father had become much wiser. Likewise, Tolstoy became much smarter thirty years after I had met him the first time. The politics and the agriculture, everything that goes on between Kitty and Levin as well as between Anna and Vronsky—it was life itself. Graham Greene was only partially right when he said that we learn about love and pain by reading. We also need to know about them *before* we come upon them again in the pages of a book. Reading opens us to new feelings, experiences, words and worlds, but we may not be ready to learn its lessons until we already have an inkling within ourselves of their truths. Art teaches in part what we already know. Just as when the student is ready, the right teacher will appear, so also books come to us when we need them.

Teachers get credit for introducing readers to books that change their lives. Sometimes the change comes accidentally; sometimes it is not for the better. We can think of daydreaming readers who lose touch with reality. Many of them are readers we are reading about: Don Quixote, Emma Bovary, both ruined by reading, or Dante's Paolo and Francesca who, reading together and sharing a book, finally put down the book ("That day we read no more") in favor of more dangerous intimacies. Petrarch warned against the dangers of reading, but did so in writing, knowing he would be read.

Reading can prepare its reader for greater, nonliterary revelations. The traditional iconography of the Virgin Mary, especially after Simone Martini's 1333 altarpiece in Siena, characterizes her as a reader, interrupted by Gabriel from her book as she is saying her prayers, then alerted via an auditory experience to something greater than her eyes can take in. Among other things, the Annunciation is a synaesthetic experience, replacing sight with hearing, in which we viewers participate by looking at someone reading and listening. Gabriel's announcement—"Hail Mary, Blessed art thou among women"—replaces one text with another. Regardless of her text (sometimes a Book of Hours, sometimes Isaiah's prediction of the virgin birth, sometimes the Song of Solomon, or the Book of Proverbs), reading signals Mary's intellectual sanctity, her closeness to God.

Reader and object reflect each other. Mary is reading about herself: what the Old Testament foretells will be realized in her life. And the New Testament will replace and fulfill the Old. In scenes of the Annunciation, the Virgin becomes her book. I am reminded of the later, unnamed secular reader in Wallace Stevens's poem "The House Was Quiet and the World Was Calm," who also "becomes" the very book he's reading. Stevens captures his reader in a piece of description rather than a dramatic interruption. The reader sinks deeper into his absorption, unlike Mary, whom Gabriel calls and turns away from her engagement. Stevens's anonymous reader becomes part of "the truth in a calm world, / In which there is no other meaning," a truth that unites reader, book, and scene. Such truth "itself / Is calm, itself is summer and night, itself / Is the reader leaning late and reading there." Wonderful verb, "to become": Stevens gives us a portrait of harmony ("My, what a becoming outfit," we say to someone) and a portrait of transformation at once. The Virgin must put down her book to receive an announcement that in some pictures terrifies her. Much depends on the depiction of Gabriel himself, either a gentle, epicene beauty or a figure who swoops in like a hawk and frightens the poor girl. She has no say in the matter. She has been chosen.

There are other stories—some descriptive and in the third person, like Stevens's, others autobiographical—about what literature means and does to its readers. My favorite is that of John Stuart Mill, who, if he is to be believed, was saved by literature itself. In chapter 5 of his *Autobiography* (1873), Mill describes his mental collapse at the age of twenty, coming on the heels of a strict education at the hands of his utilitarian father. What James Mill forgot, in his eagerness to teach his son Latin and Greek, economics and history, was to instruct him in the language of the feelings, and consequently the young man suffered what we can only label a nervous breakdown. His cure, self-administered, came via poetry, not—as he himself was surprised to learn—the poetry of the passionate, Sturm und Drang Lord Byron, but that of Wordsworth, the quiet, meditative "poet of unpoetical natures."

Mill's description is matter-of-fact and blurs the line between literary criticism, memoir, and psychotherapy:

> There have certainly been, even in our own age, greater poets than Wordsworth; but poetry of deeper and loftier feeling could not have done for me at that time what his did. I needed to be made to feel that there was real, permanent happiness in tranquil contemplation. Wordsworth taught me this, not only without turning away from, but with a greatly increased interest in the common feelings and common destiny of human beings. And the delight which these poems gave me, proved that with culture of this sort, there was nothing to dread from the most confirmed habit of analysis. At the conclusion of the Poems came the famous Ode, falsely called Platonic, "Intimations of Immortality" . . . I found that he too had had similar experience to mine; that he also had felt that the first freshness of youthful enjoyment of life was not lasting; but that he had sought for compensation, and found it, in the way in which he was now teaching me to find it. The result was that I gradually, but completely, emerged from my habitual depression, and was never again subject to it. I long continued to value Wordsworth less according to his intrinsic merits, than by the measure of what he had done for me. Compared with the greatest poets, he may be said to be the poet of unpoetical natures, possessed of quiet and contemplative tastes. But unpoetical natures are precisely those which require poetic cultivation. This cultivation Wordsworth is much more fitted to give, than poets who are intrinsically far more poets than he.

To today's sufferers, melancholics, and ordinary neurotics, can we safely say, Throw out your Prozac, pick up your Wordsworth? The advice would revolutionize the health industry.

Reading—I am tempted to call it "the best reading"—is endangered now not only because our culture has become visual and obsessed with images, but also, and more dangerously, because the culture has become a mass one. The most popular activities are performed in groups—music, sports, spectacular public entertainment, whereas the best readers are idiosyncratic solitaries. We have too much noise, especially when we least desire it. At the theater, at a concert, or at the movies, people behave as though they are still in their living rooms, sharing opinions that no one else wants to hear, whether loudly or quietly doesn't matter. To sit still in one place, especially in the presence of others, is a dying or at least an endangered custom. So where does this leave poor reading? Sitting alone, in quiet, in one's room: how many have the capacity to do that? Maybe very few ever have; perhaps "the best reading" has always been the professor's chimerical dream.

Even without such a dramatic formula as "Out with Prozac, in with Wordsworth," or "Out with rock orgies, in with solitude," we can point to other, quieter and measured claims for the saving power of a lifetime devoted to books. Virginia Woolf wrote the best estimate of reading and its rewards:

> I have sometimes dreamt that when the Day of Judgement dawns and the great conquerors and lawyers and statesmen come to receive their rewards—their crowns, their laurels, their names carved indelibly upon imperishable marble—the Almighty will turn to Peter and will say, not without a certain envy when He sees us coming with our books under our arms, "Look, these need no reward. We have nothing to give them. They have loved reading."
> ("How Should One Read a Book?" *The Common Reader*)

It hardly matters what you read. In youth I preferred the test of complexity (Proust, Joyce, James). In maturity I prefer the elegance of apparent clarity (Pascal, Willa Cather), of the art that hides art itself. But even what seems transparent has its opacities. All reading challenges us. "The poem must resist the intelligence, / Almost success-fully," said Wallace Stevens. Any reader knows that the adverb "al-most" is the most important word in that wise epigram. Reading proves us, in the sense that it tests us, and because in many cases it has made us who we are. Reading, the source of occasional disturbance, threat, anxiety, and a cause for questions and alarms, remains—as Woolf suggests—its own gratifying reward, its own useless pleasure.

2 Walking

It may seem a bit eccentric to cross the Atlantic by plane merely to take a walk. At least it would have seemed odd to me before and even during a recent excursion to England. But afterward, it also made logical if quirky sense. On my transoceanic return flight, with plenty of time to reflect on what the previous week had meant, I had something of a revelation. It came to me that I had gone to London because I wanted to breathe by stretching my legs; I had wanted to think on foot.

Let me clarify, first of all, what I was *not* doing. I was far from feeling like an adventurer—like, for instance, the great travel writer Patrick Leigh Fermor, who at eighteen in 1933 set out to walk from Rotterdam to Constantinople. And did. Neither did I go to London intent on making a pilgrimage, nor did I use the city as the deliberate starting-out point for one. Pilgrimages have a specific purpose as well as a geographical termination. They often involve the mortification of the flesh, or used to. Chaucer's fourteenth-century pilgrims wended their way to Canterbury in order, presumably, to seek absolution at the shrine of St. Thomas, and also to shake winter from their bodies once April's sweet showers had begun to relieve human dryness as well as natural drought. The mere taking of exercise was also beside the point for me. I could have done that at home. I must have had some nominal purposes for my trip (visiting friends, planning an academic meeting, going to some museums, seeing some theater), but I realized in retrospect that these were, at best, nugatory excuses for a deeper need. What I understood on my return flight was something that in fact had existed beneath the thin upper layer of my consciousness all along, namely, that I had gone to experience the enjoyment—unavailable to me on home ground—of strolling, to delight in what Wallace Stevens called "the pleasures of merely circulating," to act the role of the nineteenth-century *flâneur*, the walker in the city, as well as in city parks and nearby rural scenes.

Only recently have people even considered why we walk, and also where and when. When walking meant working, when it was the primary means of human locomotion, who would have cared about it? It was an inevitable part of life, not a choice. It is not, I think, pedestrian to think, or indeed to write, about walking. Doing so points to the core of who we are, and to the substance of our life this late in human history.

Several years ago I flew to San Diego for a conference. Waking up very early the morning after my arrival, I looked at the tourist brochures on the desk and realized that Balboa Park, site of the celebrated city zoo and the city's museums, a beautiful and renowned piece of urban landscape, lay three miles or so from my harborside hotel. I asked the young parking valets hanging around the hotel's front door whether it would be a pleasant walk through the city from the Marriott to the park. They looked incredulous, indeed bewildered: "Oh no, sir. We don't think you can walk there from here."

"Why not?" I replied, showing them the map. "It certainly doesn't look too far away."

"Perhaps not," they helpfully responded, "but it's all uphill and will take at least forty-five minutes."

Nothing daunted, I asked the boys whether they went to a gym. (I was reminded of a *New Yorker* cartoon of eager gym addicts getting into an elevator, on which hangs a sign that says TO THE STAIRMASTER beside the staircase they might have used instead.) The fellows allowed as they did. "Well, guys, here's a modest suggestion: you might try walking outside, in the beautiful California weather, as a substitute activity." Later in the day, having made the hike uphill, having toured zoo and museums, eaten lunch, window-shopped, and walked downhill home, I confronted the same young men and pointed out to them that I had returned safe and sound, and that they might in the future recommend to other Easterners or equivalent oddballs the walk to, as well as in, the park. They were relieved if bemused to learn that I had lived to tell the tale of my dangerous excursion. Had no one ever asked them about this before?

Like me, these college students lived in real, modern America, where by and large unhurried walking is not a possibility, except in small towns, and the larger, mostly Eastern cities (Boston, New York, Philadelphia, Washington, or Chicago) built before the age of the automobile and containing successful mass-transit systems. Soon after my San Diego adventure, I was visiting German friends in Cologne, who asked, "Why are you Americans so obsessed with going to the gym?" I had to remind them that people who go to gyms are defined, for the most part, significantly by class and income bracket. They are educated and have leisure time. But even more important is the fact that unless an American who does not live by physical labor makes a concerted effort to exercise, he gets none. My German friends, both in their mid-sixties, live on the fifth floor of a shabby but sturdy old-fashioned apartment building. It has an ancient elevator that works occasionally, so it might as well have none at all. They have walked up and down their stairs, often four and five times a day, with groceries and heavier packages, for thirty years. They do not need a gym.

Dallas, Texas, my latest residence, offers plenty of resistance to walkers. For one thing, it is big; for another, it is mostly physically unappealing; and for a third, it is hot much of the year. Taken individually, none of these obstacles should in theory prevent pedestrian activity. But combined, they make it unpleasant if not impossible to stroll about. Like many modern American cities, Dallas consists of a spiderweb of discrete residential communities, joined and intersected by freeways and large streets that often lack sidewalks, with neighborhood shopping centers as mini-nodes, enormous malls as larger nodes, and a downtown area that has survived without round-the-clock activity until just recently, when brave urban pioneers decided to repopulate it and turn it into livable space. Developers have awakened to the economic value of "mixed-use planning." Although some people now think they'd like to live where they can walk to and from dinner, the automobile is still king; people often drive from one end of a parking lot in a mall to the other. The ladies who lunch can wear Jimmy Choos or Manolo Blahniks because they don't have to walk in them; instead, they leave their car with the restaurant valet, make an entrance into a swank restaurant, and swan their way to the table.

Unlike many smaller or more temperate cities, Dallas can't even boast many bike riders other than people who mount their bikes on top of their cars and then drive to a lake or a rural park. Bicycles are largely invisible on the city streets because we have no bike paths and because the proliferation of SUVs and similar wide vehicles has meant that the daring cyclist is these days even more imperiled on the road. There is simply not enough space for both cars and bikes on the streets.

Pedestrians are somewhat less endangered. But years ago, when the local police caught sight of someone taking a leisurely stroll in a residential neighborhood, they might pull over and inquire what he was doing, and then, if that person looked at all suspicious (read: nonwhite), escort him to the proper destination. Now that we have the early-morning and late-afternoon, or pre- and post-prandial, health addicts doing their cardiovascular best, at least we see people on the streets, but a determined exerciser is not quite the same as a casual walker.

And in a city that has two seasons—summer and all the rest—and bad air quality for much of the year, there's little chance for, and almost no enjoyment in, walking to work even if one has a relatively short distance to negotiate. Except in truly arctic weather, you can always add layers of clothing for insulation and go outside for fun, but there is a limit to how much you can take off in the heat. In the land made possible by air-conditioning, one stays enclosed within cars, offices, homes, and even gated communities. Self-protection is the point, and it produces isolation. We shun exposure and mingling in favor of safety. Rebecca Solnit, whose book *Wanderlust: A History of Walking* (2000) offers a marvelously capacious guide to the physical and literary terrain, ignores weather as a factor that contributes positively to, as well as inhibits, the pleasures of this most natural activity. She lives in California, not Texas. Even people in Dallas who live close enough to walk from home to work cannot do so because for almost half the year they'd arrive moist and sticky.

Like walking *to* a destination, walking in order to build up heart rate and to break a sweat is just not the same as walking, pure and simple. Immanuel Kant defined art as *"Zwecklichkeit ohne Zweck"* ("purposefulness without purpose"), and the art of walking, like the other, more permanent arts, often has no function other than itself. At the same time, even to call it an art is to exaggerate its status: everyone knows how to do it, and no one after the age of two requires training in the doing, just in the wanting to do it. Babies do not have to be taught to walk. Some biological or genetic mechanism awakens them, around the end of their first year, to want to stand, pull themselves up by their arms in the crib, and turn their fat little legs into agents of mobility. They fall down; they get up; they toddle; they're off and running. What does it mean to be a good or excellent walker? That you go faster or farther than everyone else? Unless you are a race-walker, there's no point in trying to perfect or improve your walking. Even more, every new walk both repeats and varies previous ones. You cannot cross the same street twice. The American poet A. R. Ammons observes in "Corsons Inlet," "Tomorrow a new walk is a new walk," even if over the same territory. For Ammons, meandering through the sandy terrain of southern New Jersey, a dune is as much an event in time—it always changes its shape owing to wind and weather—as in space.

Neither weather nor distance nor the certain fact of unappealing vistas or tedious sameness ever got in the way of Ammons or Kant, who famously never left his home town, Königsberg, but strolled up and down in it every day. Nothing prevented Søren Kierkegaard in Copenhagen from walking and thinking. "When I have a problem I walk, and walking makes it better," the dour philosopher remarked. In a letter to his niece Jette he goes on: "Do not lose your desire to walk; every day I walk myself into a state of well-being and walk away from every illness; I have walked myself into my best thoughts, and I know of no thought so burdensome that one cannot walk away from it." Walking cleanses, clears, provokes, and repairs the mind.

Nor did climate or routine prevent America's two most famous poet-walkers from trekking back and forth between work and home. Wallace Stevens diligently walked the miles from house to insurance office in downtown Hartford, all the while composing poems in his head. Later on, Howard Nemerov walked to classrooms and office at Washington University from his suburban St. Louis home, observing acorns, foliage, neighborhood dogs, changes in the weather, and the daily round of ordinary life that became the substance of his poetry. Even in company he seldom spoke when walking. His colleague the philosopher Richard Watson remembers: "[Nemerov] used to walk home from the university with my wife Pat (a professor of anthropology) and not say a word until they parted, when he always said 'whup whup, always a pleasure,' and shambled off." Earlier, at Bennington College in Vermont, Nemerov went walking with the novelist Bernard Malamud and, according to Watson, "They used to take long walks together, almost every day, and Howard never said a word. [Malamud] said it disconcerted him at first, but Howard would nod and obviously enjoy the walks, 'so I just babbled on.'" The scholar

Roger Gilbert has written an entire book, *Walks in the World*, on the subject of poets walking. They do not—at least primarily—walk for cardiovascular health. They walk in order to compose their thoughts, a process involving both Nemerov's witty observations and Stevens's deeper, more abstruse ones. Paul Klee said of his paintings: "I take a line out for a walk." Alexander Calder might have said the same thing about his mobiles and stabiles, taking a wire and extending it into three-dimensional fullness. The English artist Richard Long took Klee's aphorism literally when he created his *Line Made by Walking* in 1967; he drew a line with his feet, so that walking became the actual medium as well as the subject of his art.

Especially those artists who work with words and ideas instead of material objects know how thinking and moving occupy separate but parallel spheres. Instead of taking a line out for a walk, poets take a walk in order to get a poetic line, or all the lines of entire poems. The process of the walk involves mind, body, and breath (literally: the spirit) in a harmonious process that at once releases and excites different kinds of energy. Wordsworth, who always hated the act of taking pen in hand to write—he became literally nauseated—used to pace in his garden, up and back, composing in his head, thereby creating an analogy between the turns of his body and the turns of lines of verse. And it was surely no coincidence that Coleridge stopped writing iambic pentameter blank verse, that basic English rhythm, when he stopped walking for pleasure.

Strolling used to be an American custom, but hasn't been for a long time. It still remains a powerful one in most European countries, especially in the Mediterranean, where an afternoon siesta makes sense during the heat of the day, followed by a reawakening in the evening, and then a promenade, a *passeggiata* or, in Germanic countries, a *Spaziergang*. The courtship ritual of the *paseo* allows young couples to be alone in public. Wandering one late Sunday summer afternoon on the Janiculum Hill in Rome, I noticed that amid the strollers— young and old, fat and thin, single, in couples, and in larger groups— the only people moving at a more intense pace were the determined

American joggers, oblivious of the pine trees, the views, and the fresh air, impervious to everything except their pulse rate and the chore at hand. The soft twilight was beginning to lay its mantle upon the hills and vistas. Families were walking slowly, courteously, and arm in arm. The scene, and the view, put me in mind of Garibaldi's description of Rome as "the greatest theater in the world." Never did running seem so inappropriate, so unnecessary, so modern. Irving Berlin's song from *Miss Liberty*, "Let's Take an Old-Fashioned Walk," specified an activity that was antique even in 1948; it would be positively unthinkable today in some quarters. Ditto his "Easter Parade"–which is really a promenade, *not* a parade–immortalized in the 1948 film that ends with Judy Garland, Fred Astaire, Ann Miller and her dogs, and an MGM cast of thousands, all in fancy dress and hats, on the avenue, snapped by the photographers.

The pleasures of merely circulating, of walking in cities, are different from those of hiking, trekking, and climbing, in forests, or hills and mountains. For one thing, the activity itself is less strenuous. For another, one can walk in cities alone, whereas climbing a mountain is best done in company. For all the talk of its restorative, salubrious powers, nature can terrify in ways that the city never does. On a precociously autumnal morning one Saturday last August, I decided to take a country hike. I was in the Berkshire Hills in western Massachusetts. I drove myself to a hill I had climbed often, but not in two decades. I recalled it as undaunting, indeed easy. I parked the car, found the trail, and began the ascent. Sunshine dappled the forest paths; the painted blue blazes on trees marked the way. The air was crisp and dry. Up I went. After fifty minutes, hearing only the sounds of the wind in the trees and the murmur of the forest pines, I began to suffer from–what should I call them?–modest panic attacks or minor delusions. I asked myself, "Do bears live here? Do they attack human beings? Do they climb trees? Am I safe?"

And then my mind began racing: "Suppose I fall and sprain my ankle? No one will see me. Suppose I call out? No one will hear me. How long will it be before another human comes along? Well, I always have the cell phone." My self-reassurance didn't work. I reached into my pocket to discover that, of course, I had left the phone in the car. So much for help in crisis. By this point I had reached a stretch of the terrain that looked especially steep, slippery, and wet. Rain had fallen the night before. Although it would have been relatively easy to continue the ascent, I thought about the potentially treacherous downward return. Climbing makes few demands on someone in decent shape. You don't lose your balance. You work against gravity. Coming down is where the danger lies. You can slide, trip, take a spill and break a leg. I kept thinking of, and reversing, the famous words of the Cumaean Sibyl in Book 6 of the *Aeneid*. She calls the descent to the Underworld the easy part—after all, everyone dies—it's coming back up that requires a miracle. *"Facilis descensus Averno . . . sed revocare gradum, hoc opus, hic labor est."* A living, breathing climber knows the truth: you endure the burden and labor not going up but coming down.

So I decided to turn around. Like Wordsworth climbing the Alps at the age of twenty when on summer holiday from Cambridge, I "still had hopes that pointed to the clouds," but like Wordsworth I was disappointed. In his case, it turned out that he had crossed the Alps without knowing it and his onward path lay downward. In mine, fear pure and simple prevented me from claiming my symbolic triumph and basking on the mountaintop after my exertions.

When alone, it's better to stick to city streets.

So I go to London—as I often go to Venice, that uniquely labyrinthine city where one is always but never really lost—to take a walk. Walking through unfamiliar cities or ones only slightly known, with a map available but frequently ignored, affords a heady pleasure different from but equivalent to that won on rural jaunts. Along with Manhattan, London and Venice are the metropolises I know best. Paris is close behind them. Walking in cities offers the wonderful combination of solitude and togetherness. Being alone in a crowd means not being alone at all, except in the caverns of one's own consciousness. The mind works constantly, but it has always seemed that the thoughts that come to me on my feet are somehow sharper, more interesting, and more surprising than others that come, say, in the car or the shower. On Memorial Day last year, walking alone in New York City, I had a vivid flash and then a reminder of a comparable day exactly twenty years earlier, when two friends and I took off from Manhattan in a convertible on a bright and sunny holiday morning, drove across the East River through Queens to Brighton Beach and Coney Island, took a wrong turn, and ended up on the Verrazano Narrows Bridge, landed in Staten Island, and said, "What the hell, we've been to four of the five boroughs," and then drove home via the Bronx just to be able to say that we'd *done* all of New York on a beautiful day in an open car. Our driving escapade was the exact opposite of a walking experience, but it now lives doubly in my mind (as the original and then in the subsequent epiphany): the sameness of weather brought about a Proustian recollection, years later, on foot. Another car ride probably would not have had the same effect. Slowness fits the mind's operations much better than speed.

And walking alone, rather than with a partner, gives the double pleasure of setting and then changing the pace, instead of compromising. You go at your own speed, not someone else's. You can make unapologetic last-minute, arbitrary, if not downright mercurial, adjustments in direction or purpose. You wander with the uncertainty of the wind itself, but ever grounded by the asphalt and the surrounding architecture. You want to pop into a shop? Feel free. You want to take a sudden turn down a tempting alley? Go ahead. Sit in a café for no reason? Not a problem. You want to go out of your way and cross a bridge just to take in the view from the other side and then come back? No one will stop you. You are the conductor, the boss. "He travels fastest who travels alone," said Robert Louis Stevenson, and that goes for mere city walks as well as more exotic peregrinations. Slow or fast: you set your own pace because you have embarked on the adventure that is life in miniature.

Only recently in Western history have cities been safe and clean, undangerous and therefore appealing to leisure walkers. In the eighteenth century few people walked the city streets for pleasure. You took your life in your hands whenever you stepped out of doors. Garbage and thieves abounded. Cities were unsavory. At the beginning of that century, John Gay's "Trivia: or the Art of Walking the Streets of London" is full of admonitions. At the end of the same century, in "London," William Blake lists the sights and, even more powerfully, the sounds of the city, none of them agreeable: "marks of weakness, marks of woe," "the mind-forg'd manacles," "the chimney-sweeper's cry," "the soldier's sigh," and "the youthful harlot's curse." Much of the horror still exists, of course, although pushed off to peripheries along with other signs of loucheness and ugliness, and many major urban destinations have developed a kind of theme-park approach to tourism. Think of Times Square.

Still, what excites is the combination of the ordinary and the unexpected. Rebecca Solnit cites the "anonymity, variety, and conjunction, qualities best basked in by walking," that cities offer. To these I'll add a fourth one: surprise. There is pleasure in being in a new neighborhood that looks in part like one's own but is of course foreign, instead. And then the conjunction of sameness and difference has an additional thrill. A bakery in St. Louis is not the same as one on the Île St.-Louis in Paris, even if they have almost identical pastries. Coincidences and human encounters occur as frequently on foreign and familiar terrain, but the ones abroad always outlast the domestic ones in memory.

In London I recalled Virginia Woolf's Mrs. Dalloway, who strides out one fine June morning to buy the flowers for her party and breathes in the intoxicating mixture of freshness and beauty from a day in spring. Any tourist to London can experience a rich synaesthetic brew of enticements. "I love walking in London . . . Really it's better than walking in the country," Clarissa says to her friend Hugh Whitbread, whom she runs into in Westminster. Mornings are best. A morning walk offers the excitement and promise of a new day, with the sun rising, and the possibility of surprise, of chance encounters with friends. Mornings betoken hopefulness. On the other hand, even Henry David Thoreau, American apostle of the a.m., had something interesting to say about nighttime walking. He found it "necessary to see objects by moonlight as well as sunlight, to get a complete notion of them." In his journal Thoreau wrote that at dusk "I begin to distinguish myself, who I am and where . . . The intense light of the sun unfits me for meditation, makes me wander in my thought." In dewy mist, "I seem to be nearer the origin of things"; in open moonlight, "our spiritual side takes a more distinct form, like our shadow which we see accompanying us." In the woods, in the country, walking at night or in shadow inspires meditation, contemplation, and self-knowledge. In the bustle of the city by day you are more likely to lose yourself and all thoughts of self. Everything is surface; there is no depth, just variety. You are engulfed by, and in touch with, the world beyond you, the world that doesn't care about your presence at all.

But, as though I were taking a walk, I digress. Mrs. Dalloway was ambling on home ground. I was not. For someone like me, so long resident in Texas, the mere fact of lilacs in redolent bloom and chestnut trees in stately blossom (both species unavailable in Dallas) gave promise of sensuous bliss. Did I go to London just to see some trees? Maybe. Familiar from childhood but now also exotic after my years of exile, the aromatic lilacs and great-rooted chestnuts touched me. "In the triumph and the jingle and the strange high singing of some aeroplane overhead was what she loved; life; London; this moment of June": this is Woolf's homage to the moment when everyone turns out of doors, whether after a wet winter or, like Mrs. Dalloway, after the horrors of a world war. Mild temperatures, the always present possibility of mist and rain, the necessity of layering one's clothing (put the slicker on, take the slicker off; open the umbrella, close the umbrella) all mean that an English walk will be a physical activity engaging many somatic conditions.

In the same way that Central Park is Manhattan's greatest work of art, so Hyde Park, Kensington Gardens, Regent's Park, and the other large greenswards in central London give nature a chance to take hold within urban life: *rus in urbe*, as Horace put it. Hyde Park is democratic, vast, and open, with playing fields and riding paths, joggers as well as strollers, people going somewhere purposefully and other people going nowhere; fast or slow, it matters not. Russell Square and smaller Bloomsbury quadrangles with fountains and sculptures also provide seasonal verdure, odors that combat the traffic fumes, and much-welcome benches. On a still smaller scale, and in a different way, the mysterious quiet of enclosed London residential squares that only key holders may enter gives one tempting visible access to spaces one cannot penetrate.

These inaccessible private squares serve as oases of calm a block or so from major thoroughfares. One wanders away from the Victoria and Albert Museum, away from the bustle of the Old Brompton Road, and finds oneself in Onslow or Harrington Gardens, or The Boltons, gardens and squares that seem to be of another time as well as of an entirely different physical dimension. One becomes aware of a spatial rhythm as one moves from enlarged, open, and commercial areas to private, domestic ones. This rhythm is perhaps even more noticeable in Paris, in which the sumptuous dignity of Haussmann's *grands boulevards* intersects with the intimacies of smaller streets leading away from them and into tranquil side pockets that always feel like culs-de-sac even if they are not. And, especially as twilight begins to descend in either of these cities, one has the related pleasure of catching glimpses of the life within the houses, of furnishings, paintings, and sometimes the residents themselves, who have unintentionally made themselves available to the passerby.

As a spectator one takes part vicariously in the lives of others. One imagines what it might be like to be inside. The window into a room is also a mirror of one's finest, profoundest dreams and aspirations. It occurred to me that a single person inside looking out is inevitably more isolated than the single person outside looking in. All the lonely people in Edward Hopper paintings, alienated and alone even when in clusters, inhabit interior spaces. Being cut off—from an enclosed garden or a glowing, fire-lit parlor—encourages compensatory feelings of imaginative warmth. The simultaneous sense of community and singularity comes clearest in urban settings.

The American poet Amy Clampitt, airplane-averse, traveled whenever possible by bus. It was a way, she said, of being alone with other people. A solo walk through a cityscape can give the sense of invisibility—Emerson's "transparent eyeball" on Concord Common and Christopher Isherwood's "I am a camera" in *Berlin Stories*—at the same time that it nurtures you with the satisfaction of mingling with the throng. Just brushing up against other people at street corners ensures greater human contact than a lifetime of commuting in air-conditioned cars, their windows constantly rolled up. Basking alone while walking in the company of strangers is the moving equivalent of a stationary Quaker meeting. It increases both inner awareness and an imaginative sympathy with, and for, other people. Like dancing, walking becomes an exercise in civility. You encounter people, friends or more generally strangers; you deal with them; you defer to them, open a door for them, or help the old lady step off the curb at the traffic light. You yield, you give way when passing or crossing a street. You are more likely to demonstrate such courtesies on foot than when strapped into the two-ton piece of metal known as an automobile. Road rage doesn't really have a pedestrian equivalent. Yes, you can bump into someone on the street and get momentarily riled, but it's unlikely that you'll pull a gun on someone who has cut you off or passed into your lane. Politeness walks; it doesn't speed.

Like all travel, by whatever means, walking signifies change. In the same way that one experiences the commonplace and the exotic simultaneously or in swift succession, one can also revise oneself when traveling. Such reinvention, or even modest self-modification, may never get beyond the limit of one's own consciousness. It's another splendid advantage of traveling alone: you can remake yourself. You can adopt a disguise without even putting on a wig or changing clothes. You pretend to yourself that you are a different person. And there is amusement to be had—as I have often found—in wandering into art galleries in New York or London's New Bond Street, or anywhere else in Mayfair, and pretending to be a serious collector. In my case, the guise (never, I am sure, believed for even a moment) is that of a mildly eccentric and thoroughly knowledgeable Texas petromillionaire with an interest in whatever the gallery is showing. People who work in galleries are hired for, and trained to have, good manners, so they and I play a game of mutual flirtation.

Although being away from native soil is helpful, it is hardly necessary for this game. Last spring I wandered into Christie's in Rockefeller Center, then preparing for its big spring auction of nineteenth- and twentieth-century art. The place was like a museum without an entrance fee. In one room I stood eyeballing at close range a delectable Joseph Cornell box, a magic surreal world in miniature, when I glanced to my left and saw Steve Martin. I looked at him, and he at me, and there we were: two men of the world examining a potential purchase. "I'll fight you for it," I said. He smiled, leaving the field entirely to me, and we wandered off in our separate directions. I'll never know whether his outing was successful, whether he was actually in the market for something, or just—like me—looking, but his fortuitous presence certainly made my experience memorable even without a single purchase. Window-shopping doesn't cost a dime, and it's almost as much fun as buying.

The pleasure in such modest pretenses never should obscure the real fact that, as Emerson remarked, "travel is a fool's paradise." *"Coelum non animum mutant qui trans mare currunt* [Those who run across the seas change their skies, not their souls]," said Horace. You can pretend to be an art connoisseur, a millionaire, a bohemian, but wherever you go, you are still yourself. Emerson again: "At home I dream that at Naples, at Rome, I can be intoxicated with beauty, and lose my sadness. I pack my trunk, embrace my friends, embark on the sea, and at last wake up in Naples, and there beside me is the stern fact, the sad self, unrelenting, identical, that I fled from. I seek the Vatican, and the palaces. I affect to be intoxicated with sights and suggestions, but I am not intoxicated. My giant goes with me wherever I go."

As long as you are comfortable with your own giant, there's no harm done in pretending to have another, fictive one. The self—sad or happy—can accept modest, or even sometimes major, modifications, the adjustments that come from change, even if only a change of skies. The purpose of the walk is pleasure, but often with the posture, the guise, of purposefulness.

For many tourists, shopping itself represents purpose as well as purposefulness. Depending on the state of currency, Americans have gone to Europe to pick up bargains. These days it's the other way around. Italian friends tell me they've come to Manhattan, not to buy American or Japanese electronic goods, but to look for Armani and Missoni clothing that for some reason understood only by international economists is cheaper for them abroad than at home. It's easy to make fun of shoppers, but shopping constitutes a viable, important, and indeed interesting activity, so I long ago stopped turning up my nose at the large groups of my countrymen buying Wedgwood, or Harris tweeds, or Scottish cashmere, or antique silver, or whatever they wanted in Great Britain. One of the pleasures of merely circulating, as Baudelaire and Walter Benjamin well knew, is being taken in mid-stroll, captivated by some eye-catching window display that encourages the nonbuyer to look, to enter, to engage in conversation, and then, perchance, to buy. Every first-time tourist feels the need of bringing home gifts for family and friends; most sensible people have given up on this, if for no other reason that in an international, Web-based economy, there very well may be no bargains left, and certainly everything is available everywhere all the time.

Some years ago, on my first trip to Rome, I—a confirmed non-shopper in my real life—had a serendipitous experience that would never have occurred had window-peeping and then buying not been my motives. Walking down the Via Giulia, I saw a shop that sold leather goods. In the window was a selection of key rings, each of them a chain holding a leather rectangle with an embossed initial or two. I thought to myself that several of these little things—lightweight, unbreakable, and inexpensive—would make perfect gifts for a half-dozen people who might be charmed by them. For once I had forgotten my Italian dictionary, but, ever confident, I strode into the shop. *"Buon giorno, signore,"* I said to the shopkeeper, and *"Buon giorno"* came back at me. I had done my calculations, based on my Italian—equal parts restaurant menus, Dante, and opera—and then proceeded: *"Quanto costano questi anelli di chiave nella finestra?"* He looked at me blankly and shrugged. So I repeated myself, louder and more slowly. It seems ridiculous, but linguists have assured us that it's natural, universal, and, indeed, helpful. Once more the question came: *"Quanto costano questi anelli di chiave nella finestra?"* He gave still no glimmer of recognition, so I led him outside and pointed to the key rings in the window. I had figured it this way: because I knew French better than Italian (although everything ultimately becomes a kind of Esperanto when I speak), *finestra* must be the equivalent of *fenêtre*. Then there was Puccini. In the first act of *La Bohème*, Mimi is searching for her *chiave* on the darkened stairway, and in *Gianni Schicchi* the heroine sings to her *babbino caro* that she wants to go to the Porta Rossa *per comperar' un anello*. So "How much is that key ring in the window?" became in my translation a question that I thought any sensible Roman would understand.

Of course, I was wrong. As it turned out, the proper word for a shop window is *vetrina*, and the key chain is a "carry-key," a *portachiavi*. Once we understood one another and had our hearty laugh, I made my purchases, and we cemented our deal with a glass of grappa. What had begun as a *passeggiata* had turned into a modest shopping foray and then a personal encounter with a polyglot joke as its climax. I could not have been more pleased. For a literary academic with little taste for dangerous physical adventure (no trekking in the Himalayas, motorcycling across the Sahara, journeys to the poles, or even camping out under the stars for me), my most exciting travel moments occur in civilized countries where I know just enough of the language to be challenged but not enough to feel fluent. It's the perfect combination: modest discomfort and uncertainty, but never fear and trembling.

Another memory—also linguistic but not commercial—comes back to me. On my only visit to Germany, I had flown to Frankfurt from Dallas, a ten-hour trip. I waited several hours for a train, and then proceeded south in the off-season to Bayreuth in Bavaria. Checking into my hotel on a beautiful October morning and thoroughly jet-lagged, I decided not even to think about lying down, for fear of never getting up. Instead, I consulted the map and walked up the holy hill to Wagner's Festspielhaus in order to pay it homage. Then I descended back into town, whose central part is closed to automobile traffic. I rested on a bench, having already taken my bearings and put away the map I had been studying. Two German women, tourists of a certain age, approached me and asked, *"Entschuldigen Sie, aber ist das das Neue Schloss?"* *"Nein, gnädige Frauen,"* I answered, not missing a beat. *"Das ist nicht das Neue Schloss sondern das Alte Schloss. Das Neue Schloss ist um die Ecke."* *"Danke schön,"* said they, and *"Bitte schön,"* said I, after which I broke into giggles inspired by my excellent tour-guide sensibilities and my imperfectly recollected year of German 101 from decades before. I had been of use. I felt like an authority. I had made myself—sort of—at home in a place and in a language, neither of which I ever would reasonably claim to have known. And all of this because I had decided to take a walk. Who needs space travel when the adventures of ordinary life can provide so much unexpected fun? I don't.

When language changes, walking and the entire exploratory adventure also change, as the two anecdotes above demonstrate. But of all the world's cities, Venice is the one that most thoroughly engages my walking eagerness, for both the obvious, and also more personal, reasons. Even if one is semi-infirm or chooses to rely almost exclusively on gondolas, water taxis, and elevators, the feet are still the primary mode of transport. Bridges over canals are StairMasters *avant la lettre*. Pedestrian life is all that Venice affords, but the city repays the demands of walking in manifold ways. It is, of course, by now a cliché to say that the city has been frozen in time, has become a living museum if not a theme park; that it exists only as a tourist attraction or an inflated mercantile outlet whose full-time population has fallen well below 100,000; that life in La Serenissima has become a mere simulacrum; that the city has never entered the twentieth, let alone the twenty-first, century. All this is true and irrelevant. Elizabethan travelers to Venice complained of bad food and price gouging; the canals have always exuded their malodorous fumes; the *acqua alta* has become worse, and the city has been sinking for as long as anyone can remember. The aptly named Fenice opera house symbolizes the immortality of the entire city: it burns, it rises from the ashes, and then art and life go on.

Everything that can be said of Venice has been said before, including the fact that everything has been said before. But every visitor has his own story to tell, unique to him although resembling everyone else's. (A couple of years ago I was walking behind a group of Midwestern tourists who had clearly not done *any* preparatory reading. The lady in front of me turned to her companion and said with wonder, "You mean they don't have cars anywhere in Venice?") On my first trip to Venice, twenty years ago, I stayed in a *pensione* on the Zattere, overlooking the wide expanses of the Giudecca Canal. Next door a similar establishment featured a plaque announcing that Ruskin had lived there. Both of them catered primarily to the English tourist trade, and the meals—both dinner and supper—seemed to argue in favor of a culinary entente cordiale: overcooked spaghetti with canned tomato sauce followed by well-done roast beef and potatoes. Who cared? I awoke the first morning, gazed out over canal and waterscape, and said to my partner, "Oh good, it's all still there." Venice disappoints some people; its fantasyland ambience has never lost its appeal to me. On our second day at the English *pensione* we found Olga Rudge, Ezra Pound's longtime companion and now essentially his widow of fifteen years, at the noontime meal. She was small and birdlike, and although the weather was warm, she was swathed in a fur coat. Escorted by an ardent American academic grilling her for information about Pound, she seemed happy to act the role of keeper of the flame and tell her stories to anyone who would listen over coffee.

The next night, we were to dine at a recommended restaurant appropriately called La Corte Sconta, the hidden courtyard. This courtyard was hidden, all right, so much so that it was impossible to get explicit directions on how to reach it. The helpful *padrone* at the hotel told us, "Just take the Number 5 *vaporetto*, get off at San Zaccaria, and then ask someone." Obedient, we did just so. We inquired of the first person on the *riva* who looked possibly local how to get to the restaurant. "Walk down this small canal, turn right, and then ask someone," she said. And so it went: walk a hundred meters, turn left, and ask. Walk fifty meters, turn right, and ask. We made it to the restaurant, tucked far away and yet not very distant at all. Coming home, we reversed the process; it did not occur to us to leave a trail of breadcrumbs, which probably would have been eaten by pigeons before we could make use of them. On another visit, solo, I tried to find a recommended restaurant and walked for forty minutes before returning to the hotel and realizing that if I had turned left instead of right when I went out the front door, I'd have been thirty seconds away from where I wanted to go.

In his 1969 book, *Streets for People: A Primer for Americans*, Bernard Rudofsky makes the provocative point that Manhattan is not a very good, let alone spectacular, city for perambulating, precisely because of its rectangular grids. (Presumably, he'd give higher marks to old New York, everything south of Fourteenth Street, with its warren of nooks and eighteenth-century crannies.) Rudofsky prefers Italian cities with their piazzas, squares both large and small, that function as havens, or gathering points that offer people openness, camaraderie, and community between the times of their linear movement through streets. By this standard, Venice must be Europe's most civilized city, not just in Piazza San Marco, which Napoleon called the world's greatest drawing room, but also in all its smaller squares, where children play soccer, grandmothers gossip and keep watch over their flock, tourists rest their weary feet, everyone eats ice cream, and in good weather takes the sun after being shadowed in narrow passageways. "Now a landscape, now a room," Walter Benjamin called Paris in his famous essay on Baudelaire. In the Mediterranean, especially in warm weather, the boundaries between outdoors and indoors become permeable. Public and private spheres mingle happily; family life can be lived out of doors, consequently making "private life" something of an oxymoron.

If the Venetian *campi*, or squares (never actually square, of course), large ones like the Campi Santa Margherita and San Polo, and smaller, vest-pocket ones, provide opportunities for sociability—either experienced or merely observed—other open spaces in Venice expose you to gloom, isolation, and existential coldness. It's always easy to get away from it all, even in such a small city. Once you move out of the major tourist venues—from San Marco, the Accademia, the Rialto, the train station—Venice is nothing but small enclaves and relatively bare spaces with a combination of ordinary domestic life and silent vistas, houses that appear empty, human life either locked within or long departed. The Castello district with the Arsenale to the east of San Marco is a relatively flat, open space with a single straight thoroughfare, Via Garibaldi, Napoleon's effort at city planning, which looks like any modest shopping street in any Italian city. Especially in the northern reaches of the city, along the Fondamenta Nuove in Cannaregio, Tintoretto's home parish, one gets a sense of exposure to the elements: the lagoon stretches far and wide. Such exposure comes often as a relief from the claustrophobia many people feel within the city's maze. It also reminds one of real life.

Enormous tourist boats fill the basin of San Marco and line the mouth of the Grand Canal. Big freighters and other commercial vessels pervade the Giudecca Canal and the northern expanse of the lagoon, giving onto the industrial city of Mestre on the mainland, the home of many of the people who actually work in Venice. The spatial rhythm I noted in London exists both more spectacularly and more subtly in Venice, and often moves in an opposing way. In London one often seeks the cool respite afforded by small parks and squares, even if they are exclusive, gated, and forbidden, as a way of avoiding city bustle. In Venice one often wants expansiveness, busyness, and—yes—signs of normal life. On my first Venetian trip I took the *vaporetto* to the Lido, not just to walk along the beach and see the casinos, but also to get a modest dose of urban modernity. The island of the Lido has streets. And trees, and lawns. It has cars! It made me feel a little ungrateful, even coarse, at the time, but I have never been happier to be reminded of Henry Ford's internal combustion engine: smelling the gasoline fumes, I felt I was breathing in the air of real life, and I could then return to the rarefied precincts of Venetian museums, Gothic *palazzi*, Palladian churches, and tiny passageways with comfort and assurance. Even in San Marco, however, the new age has made its incursions. One June day several summers ago, I was strolling near the Ducal Palace overlooking the basin and came upon an American-style spin class, led by an aggressive man barking orders to anyone who wanted to rent a stationary bicycle, listen to blaring rock music, watch his two voluptuous Spandex-suited, bike-pedaling female assistants onstage, get a major workout, and sweat a lot. So much for an old-fashioned promenade.

We think of Venice as a boisterous place, a fleshpot, a gambler's paradise, the city of carnival, masks and masquerades, of Robert Browning's "dear dead women, with such hair too," the famed courtesans of centuries gone by. Venice bade farewell to these women, and to the flesh, a long time ago. Its only real temptations—spectacularly sufficient—appeal to the eye and to the mind. More than a living city it resembles a necropolis, in the raised cemetery on the separate island of San Michele and in the *memento mori* of real figures—the inevitable beggars—as well as in fictive death-in-life ones like those in *Don't Look Now*, Nicholas Roeg's eerie 1973 film, or like Thomas Mann's Gustav von Aschenbach in *Death in Venice*, longing for Tadzio and succumbing to self-delusion, madness, and then dissolution on the Lido. Venice exudes sadness, and not only in winter or under conditions of fog. Night-walking in Venice is different from anywhere else. What seems sinister or louche in art—in Luchino Visconti's *Senso* and almost all other films set in Venice, as well as in all the historical literature—has long since vanished.

On my first trip I was alone one evening, walking as though through a ghost town. Literally so: everyone goes to Venice in the day, but by night it has emptied out. Even if one were looking for erotic adventure, there would be none to be found. It's a day-tripper's destination. Of course, some tourists spend the night, but the hotels are expensive, and many economical travelers prefer to stay on the mainland and come over in daylight. Venice's quiet is reassuring, however, rather than creepy, even in the dead of winter. Some of this quality has to do with scale: you seldom look across wide expanses of the sort you might see if you were in the middle of Hyde Park at night. Even in Piazza San Marco at its most bare, "beauty breaks in everywhere," as Emerson once observed of nature, not culture. One February night I sat in the Caffè Florian looking out at a dusting of snow on the piazza: it was like watching a confectioner add sugar to a cake. Wherever you gaze, even after windows have been shuttered, there's always some modest sign of human life, a light behind a curtain or a screen. You hear footsteps behind you in a dark corner and you feel at ease rather than threatened. Emptiness exists on a reassuringly human rather than a fearsomely cosmic scale.

Venice is a maze, a labyrinth, but one without a center. The pleasure of random wandering comes in large part from the knowledge that eventually you'll get where you are going—even or especially if not right away. Venice-as-maze engages rather than frustrates. Wherever you are you will see signs that say TO THE RIALTO, TO SAN MARCO, TO THE ACCADEMIA, or TO THE RAILWAY STATION. It is as impossible to get lost as it is to find your destination. There are no straight lines, no direct routes, and shortcuts are known only by the old-timers. Even if you know your way from one place to another and you make the choice or the mistake of venturing down a previously unexplored alley or passageway, you'll get lost and find out that there are no parallel routes. It's not the same as going down Fifth Street instead of Seventh Street. "You can't get there from here," as they say, but of course you can, and eventually you do.

One cold February night, attending a cultural conference near Piazza San Marco but staying with friends near the Frari, I was walking home late, alone. I thought I had memorized the proper turns, but evidently I had gone astray. I saw a light in a small local taverna. I walked in and said to the barkeeper, *"Buona sera, signore; io sono perduto."* *"Ma no,"* he helpfully replied. *"Lei non è perduto. Lei è qua!"* "You're not lost! You're here!" He was right: I was *there*, and *there* turned out to be right around the corner (if "corner" is the correct word) from where I was supposed to be. I was coming from the opposite direction. North, south, right, left are meaningless ideas in Venice, even in daylight, when it's all but impossible to take one's bearings by the sun, which is often hidden by roofs, towers, and narrow streets. One salutary brandy later, I left the bar, turned the corner, and was home.

Time, "ever that Everest among concepts," according to the late James Merrill, exists in any person's life in both a linear and a circular way. Each of us moves forward from cradle to the inevitable end. Every life is like a walk: some follow a more-or-less straight path, while others take unexpected, unpredictable turns. Some paths *are* direct, others *seem* direct, and still others merely ramble. Directions are clear only ex post facto. Time also exists in circuits, like those walks that we take every day, repeating the same steps but with different observations and under different conditions. We leave home, we go out, we land elsewhere, and then mostly we return home. Constant, repeated movement is our daily progress, even though repetition can often fool us into thinking that we are going nowhere fast. "The Pleasures of Merely Circulating," one of Wallace Stevens's faux-nursery-rhyme poems, begins with the music of a round:

The garden flew round with the angel,
The angel flew round with the clouds,
And the clouds flew round and the clouds flew round
And the clouds flew round with the clouds.

What sounds like sheer tedium, in rhythm, rhymes, and repeated words, Stevens calls "pleasures." As I remarked at the start of this essay, pedestrian life gives access to greater than pedestrian experiences. The ordinariness of the daily round opens us to discoveries of self and world. The garden moves with the angel, the angel with the clouds, and finally the clouds dissolve into one another. Stevens has begun what looks like a list, something linear, which then turns in upon itself, undoing our expectation of something greater. From garden to angels to clouds: we are waiting for something else to follow "clouds," something like "and the clouds flew round with the heavens," but it's clouds all the way, in a gentle, nebulous intensity. They are like us. Always on the move, always flying "round" like the clouds, we are never lost because we are going nowhere, fast or slow it doesn't matter. As the bartender said to me that cold February night in Venice, we are *here*, wherever that may be.

3 Looking

ometimes you fly across the ocean to take a walk. Sometimes you fly across the country to see an exhibit. And, just once, you fly to New York to take a walk in Central Park, where the smartest, latest art show is on view. Walking and seeing: an inevitable combination. It's virtually impossible—not to say dangerous—to walk with your eyes closed. You have to see something, after all. Looking is another matter.

In February 2005, I flew, I walked. I saw, and I looked at Christo's *The Gates*, that mostly well-received site-specific work of art with a two-week life span. It provoked its share of doubters and naysayers, who wagged their heads as if noticing the emperor in his new clothes or who worried about adverse ecological damage to Central Park. For the most part, it energized and delighted onlookers. It was art in time as well as space, a case of sameness and variety, constancy and change, theme and variations. By now, like most things in time, it has disappeared from historical consciousness except from the minds of most of the tens of thousands of visitors who walked through the park—both the New Yorkers who do so every day and the travelers who came specifically to do so during these weeks—and saw, smiled, frowned, furrowed their brows, shook their heads, and chatted happily with other people doing exactly the same thing. In the late sixties we had Be-Ins; in 2005 we had a Walk-Through. For sixteen days during the year's grayest, chilliest month, people looked up, down, and at, walked beneath and talked about, the 7,500 gates, all festooned with saffron panels. Ranging from five and a half to eighteen feet wide, *The Gates*, inspired by the red torii gates in Kyoto's Fushimi-Inari-Taisha, wound their way along twenty-three miles of paths in the park, and people did the same.

The Gates was neither beautiful nor complicated, not in any simple sense of those terms. It looked like seemingly endless eye candy, but it was also more. It changed constantly, responding to sun and shadows, wind, rain, and clouds. Lucky residents of buildings on all four sides of the park got to watch it *de haut en bas* from their windows and balconies, looking through the leafless branches of the trees down to where the banners made a new and unexpected pattern, an orange design rather than the green and lacy canopy of summer's beauty. Like Wallace Stevens's famous jar placed upon a hill in Tennessee ("Anecdote of the Jar"), *The Gates* changed the park, and spruced it up. Stevens called his hill a "slovenly wilderness." Central Park was never that, of course, but Olmstead and Vaux's 1858 plan for a greensward had a makeover or at least a facelift. *The Gates* was an occasion for looking and for thinking. Adults and children, all aesthetes-in-training, debated the Big Questions: Is This Art? Is This Good Art? How Do You Know? Socrates would have felt at home. Never have so many people in Central Park talked to absolute strangers. *The Gates* became Manhattan's own Athenian *agora*, a place and an occasion for human interaction. It gave many people an extra lift in their step.

It also made me think about why we focus our eyes on the extraneous and the transient. Life is supposed to be short, and art long, but the life of *The Gates* was like that of the mayfly. "Death," said Stevens in "Sunday Morning," "is the Mother of Beauty." We looked at *The Gates* because we knew we would be around long after it had come down. Across the world today there are thousands of people who received one-inch-square snippets of fabric from the material that went into *The Gates*. Many of them, like me, must have framed their tiny mementos. These, along with our photos and our mental images, constitute our collective souvenir. *The Gates* was performance art, both by the makers, Christo and his wife, Jeanne-Claude, and by the spectators who became part of the action. Looking melted into doing. Central Park was a stage set, and all of us were the actors.

Looking gives pleasure. It also inspires. In a letter dated September 21, 1819, John Keats wrote to his friend John Hamilton Reynolds: "Somehow a stubble field looks warm—in the same way that some pictures look warm—this struck me so much in my Sunday's walk that I composed upon it." Such a condensed, confident, abbreviated sentence introduces the author's last important poem, the valedictory "To Autumn." Seeing the autumnal fields in Winchester reminded Keats of paintings, and inspired one of his greatest works. Looking is creative action, and it generates other kinds of creativity. Not only did Keats "compose" upon the scene, but we may also say that the scene offered him the serenity, the composure, of viewing it.

A painting recently stopped me, quite literally, in my tracks, and inspired me to write a poem, the first of my adult life. Between the effusions of late adolescence and this moment, I had never thought or dared to do such a thing. But here I was, in the museum. I stopped, I was challenged, I composed. I rose to the occasion, and in composing I composed myself. The moment occurred in front of Edward Hopper's 1957 *Western Motel*. Not only did the picture look warm to me, but also, with great immediacy, it put me in mind of a line of Shakespeare: "She sat, like Patience on a monument." I rewrote the line, changing its punctuation. And then I thought of another, and then another. I am not Keats, but I was heated up. I didn't stop.

Western Motel is the only picture by Hopper in which a human figure looks directly out at the audience. Most of his people look down, away, aslant, or they hide their faces from us. Here a woman sits erect on a motel bed, with a Buick's front end nosing its way into the scene right outside a large plate-glass window, beyond which lie low menacing hills just on the other side of the street. She looks impassive, cold, and perhaps uncertain. On the floor her two packed bags sit beside the bed. Rusted-orange draperies, a sea-green wall, a burgundy dress, provide a garish sense of color. The woman's blue jacket lies across a chair. On the right side we see part of the motel room's door. In spite, or perhaps because, of the large window—which clearly does not open—and the transparence with which it gives on to the waiting finned coupe, the scene suggests both light and heat, expansiveness and entrapment. In fact, we have no idea whether the woman has just checked in or is waiting to check out. And is she alone, or perhaps waiting for a man—husband? lover?—to join her, or to take the bags out to the car? The frame of the glass window, like the frame of the painting, tends to stifle, to suffocate, both her and us, her viewers. Where has she come from? Where will she go? With whom?

Like all Hopper's best paintings, *Western Motel* inspires us to ask questions and to provide tentative answers, to imagine or to write little stories about a scene, about one or more characters, his people caught in lonely postures or engaged in the trivial daily activities that constitute the bulk of anyone's life. A picture suggests a vignette. Keats also asked questions and wanted answers, which never came, in the "Ode on a Grecian Urn": "What men or gods are these?" "Who are these coming to the sacrifice?" Hopper's bright picture had me in its thrall. Looking at it, and especially at the woman with her regal posture, perfect oval face, and blank expression, I said to myself, "She sits. Like Patience on a monument? / Not quite." The allegorical figure in *Twelfth Night* sat "like Patience on a monument, / Smiling at grief." Hopper's painted woman is unsmiling and uncomplaining, perhaps desperate, perhaps on the verge of speech. Is she saying, "Take me out of here"? Or "Thank God we've come in from the desert heat and the air-conditioning works just fine"? Paintings cannot speak, and whatever we infer about people in the paintings, they cannot speak either. We animate them with language, putting our words into their mouths.

Adjectives kept flooding down on me about this woman and her situation: "stiff," "reclusive," "stern," "opaque," "stolid," "cryptic." The picture was making demands upon me, and I responded in ninety lines of blank verse. The woman and her surroundings—everything that Hopper had used to place her in a scene—provoked me, first by putting me in mind of a single line of verse and then by inspiring me to go on, to continue with my ruminations and with my lines.

"Western Motel," my maiden speech, is not "To Autumn," but it is not bad for a first poem written after more than forty years. It does not reach the level of sophisticated refinement of many poems in what we call the ekphrastic mode, which deal with a visual stimulus like a picture and speak to or about it, or sometimes through it. (In the famous climax to his ode, Keats endows his urn with consoling words: "Beauty is Truth, Truth Beauty: That is all / Ye know on earth and all ye need to know.") But it evinces the way one can be halted and gripped by a painting, and can "come to one's senses"—wonderful phrase!—with a provocation to look harder at what one is seeing. Hopper brought me to a scene of looking, and to the sense of looking as well. When you look hard at something, Gerard Manly Hopkins wrote in his notebooks, it begins to look hard right back at you.

Aristotle says that we like looking at pictures of things that, in real life, would repel or disturb us—snakes, corpses—because pictures give pleasure that real life denies us. This chapter is about the pleasures of seeing and the happiness that comes from looking, mostly but not exclusively, at pictures, even abstract ones that appeal to us precisely because they don't represent or imitate anything, because they give us something denied by real life.

I was not always a good looker, and certainly not a born one. I had no eye for color or design; as a kid I neither doodled nor painted nor made mounds of clay. If asked what sense most defined me, I would have to say "hearing." Speech and music, the first with its possibility for communicable meaning, the second with no meaning but with variations in tone, drew me in. I played the piano. Any shaping I did was with words. My eye was essentially a passive organ, letting me see where I was going but not necessarily making me take it all in. I probably bumped into a lot of walls and trees on my way home from school. I still do. Years later, I was struck by Wordsworth's claim for the eye as the most despotic of the senses. Smell, touch, and taste are primary, primitive, and instinctual according to neonatologists and pediatric psychiatrists. Among the senses, sight develops last, but when it does, it overwhelms us. Wordsworth wasn't kidding. In "Tintern Abbey" he says that his memory of a favorite spot in nature and the "forms" it has left imprinted in his mind "have not been to me /As is a landscape to a blind man's eye." What exactly does this mean? A person blind from birth can learn the word "landscape." The thing itself can be explained but not quite understood. It exists as an abstraction. On the other hand, someone who goes blind later in life retains some cognitive memory of the visual realm; a landscape becomes part of the arsenal of those things that bind him to the world and to his earlier self. For Wordsworth, the "bodily eye," that organ connecting us to external reality, is a dangerous taskmaster. It holds us captive.

It may also free us. Many people—sensitive in other ways—have no interest in the visual arts. Graham Greene and Evelyn Waugh were impervious to and took little pleasure in looking. But then the speaker of Anthony Hecht's poem "The Venetian Vespers" says, "I look and look, as though I could be saved simply by looking." For the rest of us, I might ask, What are the processes of looking that capture and then save us? What are the pleasures of scrutiny?

The first pictures I recall looking at rather than simply seeing were the seascapes of Raoul Dufy and the cityscapes of Maurice Utrillo, all shown in reproduction by our eager, earnest, seventh-grade teacher trying to enlighten her savage suburban twelve-year-old charges. I had no idea that the experts held these painters from the School of Paris in low regard, that the play of light and shadow, the bright washes of color, the quick flicks of the wrist that brought the paint to the canvas were all tricks learned from Matisse, Monet, and the greater Impressionists. I thought this is what beauty meant. One can do worse than to introduce the visual arts with "pretty" pictures. Within a year or two, I had a poster from the Philadelphia Museum of Art over my bed: Picasso's 1906 *Woman with Loaves*. We had made a class trip in ninth grade. As I looked at it, something in the picture looked back at me. My taste was being formed, although I probably could not have articulated how or why at the time. The appeal of the painting had something to do with its muted colors, gentleness of characterization, and, above all, with balance: the woman's balance of the tilted loaves on her head; the symmetry of her elongated and mysteriously calm face. It's a study of repose, a human still life, a coolly colored snapshot of arrested movement. From this point on, as it turned out, my favorite pictures would share the qualities of *luxe, calme, et volupté*. However moving I find Caravaggio, his chiaroscuro and dramatic action, his Saul of Tarsus thrown from his horse, and St. Peter crucified upside down, I return to still lifes, to Chardin, Cézanne, Morandi, and William Bailey. Whatever life was like, I must have thought, painting was its opposite as well as its complement. I want painting that composes me.

I wandered into an art class during my junior year at college, half thinking that I needed to "expand my horizons" (an apt though clichéd metaphor) and fulfill a requirement at the same time. For reasons long forgotten, probably something having to do with scheduling, I skipped over the introductory course and just plunged into the Italian Renaissance. The classes on architecture and sculpture left me bored or baffled, perhaps because reducing three-dimensional works to the two dimensions of slides inevitably eviscerates them; perhaps because, without knowing it, I had entered the Clement Greenberg school of art criticism that holds that sculpture is what you back into, during a museum visit, in order to get a better or different view of a picture on the wall; perhaps because what I really cherish is the containment offered by two-dimensional representations. I never did well with the terms of architecture (architrave, bossage, cornice, crenellation, fenestration, pycnostyle, spandrels: they sounded wonderfully exotic, but exactly what they *meant* was all a foreign tongue), and I was a little hazy on the forms and materials and processes of chiseling marble, carving wood, or pouring bronze into wax molds. But pictures I could understand in my naïve way. The painter stands in front of an easel, or lies on a high scaffold, if he happens to be painting a ceiling in the Sistine Chapel, with his colors and applies the paint. The simplicity of means appealed to me.

After Masaccio and the beginnings of perspective, after Uccello and the vanishing points in *The Battle of San Romano*, after the sublime geometric purity and the chaste mysteries in the faces of Piero della Francesca's angels, which reminded me of my hometown Picasso, there came a moment blinding but equally revelatory. I don't think I exaggerate when I say that I must have gasped audibly when the professor flashed on the screen what became an instant icon to me of everything a painting can be and do: Leonardo's *Virgin and Child with Saint Anne* (1510) from the Louvre, the cartoon for which hangs in London's National Gallery. Suddenly every lesson we had learned about spatial relations, geometry, drapery, the human form, and the sculptural qualities inherent in even a two-dimensional work became clear. I sensed what Roger Fry called "significant form," how it made visible the very human connection between generations, the stream of life flowing from one mother (Saint Anne), to her daughter the other mother, and then to the child. The picture reproduced a seamless flow of energy. We were not told that Leonardo might have chosen this unusual theme for symbolic reasons. Freud either saw or imagined the shape of a vulture in the Virgin's garment, and suggested a psychoanalytical explanation: as a child Leonardo dreamed that he had been attacked in his cradle by a vulture. I doubt that psychoanalysis would have deepened or heightened my purely aesthetic appreciation of the picture, whatever it might have taught me about the painter's unconscious motivation. Then, as now, it was form—pure but never simple—that dictated my response. Art gave me what biography and history withheld.

Other revelations followed. On my first trip to London the Turner watercolors at the Tate Gallery proved that an artist could use delicacy of means to depict elemental violence. Ruskin said that Turner's underlying theme is Death, a theme rearticulated by John Berger as "solitude and violence and the impossibility of redemption." But both Turner's exterior subjects (trains, storms, seas, skies, and weather) and his interior ones (scenes from Petworth) made me conscious of abstraction and the choreographed arabesques that would lead to a love of Jackson Pollock, although I had no idea of it at the time. Ruskin also said that Turner's true subject was the "palpitating" vitality of paint; never had I been more aware of the materials of what I was looking at than its subject.

Like his oils, Turner's watercolors depict external reality. They dramatize as well the mutual control of that reality over the artist, and of him over it. Atmosphere trumps clarity; light suffuses and obliterates individual objects. A gauzy haze often undoes the bounding line. Although Turner was Britain's greatest history painter, it was his methods rather than his subjects that drew me in. He managed to invent a whole way of rendering what he saw. Francis Bacon, thinking of his own pictures a century later, said that a painter wants his work to be both factual and "deeply suggestive or deeply unlocking of areas of sensation other than simple illustrating of the object." And Giorgio Morandi, painter of bottles, those lifelong variations on a single theme, said that "nothing can be more abstract, more unreal, than what we actually see . . . Matter exists, of course, but has no intrinsic meaning of its own, such as the meanings we attach to it." I began, in my twenties, to attach meanings, that is, feelings and responses to color and form, to what I saw in pictures. Pictures began to unlock areas of sensation in me, especially nonverbal areas.

Painting affects people differently. Like Patricia Hampl, whose

Blue Arabesque meditates on a single picture of Matisse which she saw as a student, I began as a person given to language and sound, one who came to painting, and came to my visual senses, in early adulthood. Hampl's experience with Matisse left her *not* "thinking in words. I was hammered by the image." For any writer Matisse is a good choice because he's *all* form and color, texture, and beauty. His art does away with narrative, symbolism, with anything that smacks of language, meaning, or thinking. He got his sense of color from his mother, a milliner. His father was a seed merchant from a line of weavers. Hampl reminds us: "The economy of his home and of his town was predicated on the flummery of ornament and the appetite for the unnecessary. Decoration was, paradoxically, essential." Yes, I said to myself, this is what beauty is. No one *needs* a painting, just as no one needs (see chapter 4) the fox-trot or any other dance, but ornament and essence are not necessarily in opposition. The first may be simply another word for the second.

The necessity of the decorative, the ornamental, and the "inessential" appears in a thoroughly unhectoring, quiet way in Elizabeth Bishop's early poem "Filling Station." The speaker encounters a "quite thoroughly dirty" Esso station, grease-impregnated and staffed by an equally greasy and dirty father and sons. The signs of domesticity and ornament—of what we would modestly call art—are what really catch her eye:

> *Some comic books provide*
> *the only note of color—*
> *of certain color. They lie*
> *upon a big dim doily*
> *draping a taboret*
> *(part of the set), beside*
> *a big hirsute begonia.*
>
> *Why the extraneous plant?*
> *Why the taboret?*

Why, oh why, the doily?
(Embroidered in daisy stitch
with marguerites, I think,
and heavy with gray crochet.)

From looking closely, she turns to questions, and to answers. She ends by conjuring the maker, the artist, the absent mother:

Somebody embroidered the doily.
Somebody waters the plant,
or oils it maybe . . .

Somebody loves us all.

"Extraneous"? Hardly. Bishop's eye reminds her, and us, that even in the gas station the plant is necessary. I am tempted to say *especially* in the gas station, in the lives of the working poor, not the haute bourgeoisie or the idle rich. Years before reading Hampl's delicious book, I read of and agreed with Matisse's description of his dream (much derided by Marxists, Puritans, and all those whom Harold Bloom has labeled as the Resentniks) "of an art of balance, of purity and serenity, devoid of troubling or depressing subject matter, an art that could be . . . a soothing calm influence on the mind, something like a good armchair that provides relaxation from fatigue." Color is more than surface; it is essence. The lavish light of the Riviera, the dozing, nonchalant, half-sketched human figures, the explosive blues and reds and yellows of Matisse's paintings not only reflect a preference for luxury and leisure but also present a new way of seeing. Henry James said: "The mere use of one's eyes in Venice is happiness enough." One can be saved by looking, whether at a real, living scene or, indoors, at a represented one. What else should a painting do other than bring pleasure?

Some people like to think. But people like Hampl and me who spend their working lives with words, forming, shaping them into sentences, paragraphs, and then fuller articulations, often turn to painting to escape from words. The literary critic J. Hillis Miller has said that we go to literature, especially to poems, for what he calls "the linguistic moment," that instance when a poem brings language to the foreground and makes us aware of poetry's materials and methods rather than its subject. Likewise the greatest paintings make us aware of painterliness, of the means of representing something and (especially in the case of nonrepresentational and abstract work) of creating something new. Coleridge long ago distinguished between a copy and an imitation. In an ordinary copy we are first struck by the resemblance to the thing represented. In the imitation, a superior thing, it's difference we notice first. A deeper sameness comes into focus only after an initial shock. Unlike a mediocre picture, a great one acquaints us with its materials. I had learned this from Turner. The last material I want to see in a picture is language. I want something different. I do not want to think, at least not in words. I don't like a picture any more than a piece of clothing—that talks to me. The wise dance critic Arlene Croce once said that she never liked a ballet that was supposed to make her "think," that is, one with a message, an idea, or a political point. She goes to ballet for what a choreographer can do with bodies moving through space and in relation to music. That's what dance does. When she wants to think about politics, world peace, or the ecosystem, she reads the newspaper.

Here's something I noticed on a recent trip to the Museum of Modern Art. On two walls of the central atrium—that large functional space that is, at best, uncongenial for works of art—there hung four heroic abstract oils by the late Joan Mitchell from the long course of her extended career. The pictures contain vast plots and lines, whole fields of color. Mitchell called her work landscape, not action, painting, and she said that its apparent freedom was in fact totally controlled. With their radical manipulations of color and form, the pictures invite intense and close scrutiny. No one was looking at them. I stood for forty-five minutes looking at people looking around, or rather milling around. What did I see? What were they looking at? Not

Joan Mitchell, whose work was lost on the walls, just as Monet's enormous *Water Lilies* was dwarfed when it hung on one of the same walls after the museum reopened. It looked like a muddy poster in a college dorm room. So did Mitchell's pictures. The space overwhelmed them, but they were not—if you really wanted to focus on them—unviewable or unapproachable.

The museum visitors, however, were universally transfixed by *What Happened to Us?* a site-specific wall installation, a towering piece of "art lite" by a hip young Romanian artist. It was the equivalent of easy listening, all cartoons and images and words, and easy-to-swallow jibes and clichés, childish feints and gestures. And people were taking pictures of these graffiti. The wall's glibly political slant played into the current zeitgeist. Jejune navel-gazing makes no demands on its viewers. There was no hard work involved in looking, just as the so-called work of art itself gave off no hint of urgency. Time was not of the essence. And there is no great work of art that doesn't demand time from its audience.

I felt like Eliza Doolittle: "Words, words, words, I'm so sick of words." I don't want a painting to make me think; I don't need Jenny Holzer to remind me how much I am manipulated by advertising, the media in general, or the simulacra of reality in a postindustrial, postmodern society that has destroyed authenticity. I don't want messages. (When asked by an underling about the message of a proposed movie, Sam Goldwyn said that if you want a message you send for Western Union. I'm with him on that one.) It took about thirty seconds to get the full effect—inside the museum's galleries—of John Baldessari's 1966–68 painting *What Is Painting*, with its title flush left at the top and, beneath the title, in caps, this:

DO YOU SENSE HOW ALL THE PARTS OF A GOOD
PICTURE ARE INVOLVED WITH EACH OTHER, NOT
JUST PLACED SIDE BY SIDE? ART IS A CREATION
FOR THE EYE AND CAN ONLY BE HINTED AT WITH
WORDS.

Well, yes, I did sense this, but I knew it before the picture reminded me of the deep truth. In the old days, the visual arts served practical purposes. The usefulness of painting to Christian gospel was a significant reason for Giotto's frescoes, and everyone else's work in tempera, oil, and stained glass, from the Middle Ages through the Renaissance, when the Church could use religious art as a way of explaining theological stories, mysteries, and articles of faith to a largely illiterate populace, many of whom would not have understood the Latin of the Mass. That was then. This is now. We are no longer illiterate. If anything, we have lost the ability to see, to look, now that we have gained the ability to read.

"Let's get away from it all" can have different meanings. Last fall I attended an academic convention with lots of talk. Forty-eight hours of enforced congeniality, most of it pleasant, and confinement with intelligent people, many of them friends, left me with nothing to complain about but something to look forward to: silence, and then the use of my eyes instead of my ears and brain. A weekend of conversation about literature and education made me hungry for the colors and forms of pictures, for the silent wisdom of art. I made a beeline to the Art Institute of Chicago, that venerable Michigan Avenue establishment, on the Sunday afternoon after my last academic session. Crowds had assembled to see—on the final day of their appearance—three panels from Ghiberti's *Gates of Paradise*, the doors for the Baptistery in Florence. For purposes of renovation the museum had closed major wings—there was no European art before El Greco, and most of the twentieth-century American wing was in metaphorical mothballs, but I didn't care. I could feast on what there was. By some miraculous chance people seemed more polite than usual, even subdued. I heard no loud voices. No one interfered with me and my pictures. I visited old friends and I made new ones. For more than three hours I got away from it all.

A lively and life-affirming experience, looking at pictures that afternoon kept me simultaneously alert and dreaming. I was on the qui vive for whatever struck my fancy, and lots of things did. I met, for the first time, the late-nineteenth-century American Dennis Miller Bunker, a wonderful minor artist who used a heavy impasto in his silky little impression of a Normandy landscape and a village with steel-gray church spires, a scene of both calm and menace. Thick, almost clotted brushwork took an ordinary sight and deepened it. You wanted both to be in the place and to escape from it. The perfect antidote, in an adjacent room, was Sargent's double portrait of two American artist friends of his, Wilfred and Jane Emmet de Glehn, painting at the Villa Torleoni in Frascati. Working in her painter's smock, Jane is a study in white, a delicious tumult of meringue. Sargent's brush heaped layer upon smooth layer on his friend, depicting her in the act of depicting.

A move to another room: Delacroix, in the small but sumptuous Oriental action fable *The Combat of the Giaour and Hassan*, produces swirls of primary colors; Ingres, in his portrait of the Marquis de Pastoret, may trick you into thinking that the thickly textured forest-green background curtain is sheer malachite. And then there are Matisse's yellows, evoking the land where the lemon trees bloom, and making you long to join him in Nice in an airy apartment with French doors overlooking the Mediterranean and an elegant woman relaxing on the balcony.

I needed these three hours in order to decompress. After two days of literary people dressed in their standard-issue black and tweed garb, I was starved for color. I wanted to wander not so much in and out of consciousness as in and out of view of things that from a distance drew me in. There's a rhythm to museumgoing that requires silence and solitude. The ear and tongue become quiet and the eye opens, in order to feed something like the soul. I left both aroused and sated.

A painting is an object for contemplation. You must look at it and try as hard as possible to exclude everything else from your mind. This "everything" includes ambient noise and other people who walk in front of you or step on your toes. It also includes the regrettable fact that new or big museums–in the name of traffic control–don't offer adequate seating in most rooms because they want to encourage us to move through quickly. And quick movement is exactly what happens. Studies as well as commonsense observation suggest that the average viewer spends less than ten seconds in front of a picture. Then he's on to the next one. It's the indoor equivalent of bus coach tours. Many people in museums are, in fact, part of bus coach tours, dropped off for an hour or two before heading to cafeteria, gift shop, and the next stop on the day's itinerary. Inside, they have wired their ears to the audio guides; they might as well close their eyes entirely. At many museum shows, more people are perched on benches in front of the video displays–which should be preparatory or ancillary to the main attraction–than are looking closely, or long and hard, at the pictures. It's easier to get the word from the plummy-voiced Philippe de Montebello than to take in with your eye what is in front of you.

The ideal is to be alone with a painting, one at a time. I envy those people who, especially in the days when museums cost little or nothing, had the luxury of wandering in at lunch to look at a single object. It's the pause that refreshes. And that also deepens one's consciousness. Like Robert Browning's Duke of Ferrara in "My Last Duchess," who draws open the curtain to view the picture of his late wife, and thereby exercises total control over her and his audience, I want to be an epicurean of enjoyment. Last year I visited the Brera Gallery in Milan, a treasure trove of Italian painting. I had come to see two things in particular, but did not shut my eyes to others. One of my intended pictures was Piero della Francesca's late Montefeltro altarpiece. It hangs in a badly lighted room with four other pictures from the school of Urbino. No other person shared the space; no one blocked my view; no one spoke. The museum itself was fairly empty, a couple of polite British tour groups and some random single visitors wandering through. I asked the helpful, informative guard whether I might move a chair to a position right in front of the painting, which was set apart by a metal rail. He graciously allowed me to do so, and he even let me sneak for a minute behind the railing in order to get an up-close look at the brushwork. I was alone with Piero and my own thoughts. The solitude lasted twenty-five minutes before another human being wandered in. This is how pictures should be looked at.

Another time I ambled into the print room at Harvard's Fogg Museum, and the graduate students enthusiastically brought out Ingres sketches and watercolors for me alone to see. One at a time. I felt like a prospective buyer or, even better, the actual owner. I could touch the paper. It's not that I want to prevent others from looking, even if they're in the same room with me at the time. Rather, I know that the greater the audience, the greater the distraction, and viewing pictures, unlike attending a play, is not a spectator sport. Why should I have to overhear people screaming, or even speaking quietly (which they seldom do anymore), and ruining my fun? Why should I have to overhear the Acousti-guides, turned up to high volume, no matter how illuminating the speaker may be?

It's an interesting and little discussed question: How do you like going to museums, with whom, and under what conditions? Call me antisocial: I like my space, my own company, and my solitude. I don't want to feel obliged to speak to someone else or respond to someone else's observations and questions, unless the person happens to have interesting ones and knows when to back off. Visiting a museum is travel writ small. Like walking in the city, one often prefers doing it alone, in order to speed up, slow down, backtrack, sit for a moment, or break for lunch or coffee. Looking can be selfish. Why shouldn't it be? We're not at a cocktail party.

E. M. Forster, not by nature a visual person, wrote in his 1939 essay "Not Looking at Pictures" about the pleasure of the wandering look and the wandering mind: "The mind takes charge . . . and goes off on some alien vision. The mind has such a congenial time that it forgets what set it going." Looking at pictures with Roger Fry, Forster was always amused to learn that they seemed to be looking at, or for, different things, and that he always played the naïve foil to Fry's more sophisticated and well-focused eye. Occasionally their enthusiasms or visions coincided, but most of the time they made separate discoveries: " 'I fancy we are talking about different things,' he would say, and we always were; I liked the mountain-back because it reminded me of a peacock, he because it had some structural significance, though not as much as the sack of potatoes in the foreground." Forster trained himself or was taught somewhere to look for diagonal lines, and when he found one, as in Titian's late *Entombment*, he was in business. When he didn't, he got lost, as with Velásquez's *Las Meninas*, where he had to contend with waves instead of simple diagonals.

Looking, like travel, can test a friendship. You want someone who won't lecture, threaten, overwhelm, bully, or (worst of all) bore you, but you also want a resource who will give information and act as a sounding board. You want a heightened, better version of yourself, a second pair of eyes.

MoMA's atrium was not, on that particular summer day, the focus of my visit, merely a prelude to it. I had come to experience the full force of the mammoth work of Richard Serra, especially the three new giant pieces installed beyond the atrium on the museum's second floor. I came not just to see but to inhabit, because within Serra's undulating forms you find yourself, or lose yourself, in space that constantly changes, at times pressing in, at times opening up. Contraction and expansion: the bending planes of the giant steel spiral plates inspire alternating jolts of claustrophobia and exposure. A walker through the sculpture loses and then finds himself. It was like being in Venice: one was often in doubt, but never in danger.

Most people were not walking, let alone pausing; they were speeding. Even more than in the picture galleries, visitors barely registered what they were seeing. I heard a woman complain to her husband, "I feel like I'm in a submarine." At least she articulated a response; others just ran through as though they were in a carnival fun house or the tunnel of love. A better metaphor would be

Dante's dark forest, or an inward-turning seashell, a chambered nautilus, an open cave, a labyrinth with no center. But, as with *The Gates*, the viewer could become—if he waited—a participant. Serra's *Sequence*, *Band*, and *Torqued Torus Inversion* (all produced in 2006) made something happen to you. As you walked through the plates, you felt that you were in a Möbius strip, with no outside, no inside, just an enclosed path that gave onto the ceiling, with walls leaning in and out, urging you to go forward, unless you stopped to look around.

Almost no one stopped. People shot through quickly, bored, nervous, or eager to escape. The pieces cry out to be strolled through; even more, they ask you to halt in your tracks. And, when you do, you realize that the plates themselves remind you of something like the caves at Lascaux. You see designs, colors, pictures: Are they deliberate? Did Serra make incisions? Are you hallucinating? I saw a flower; a heart; a long horizontal line like a vestigial dragon or giant fish with a long tail and an open mouth; leafy shapes like fossils embedded in stone; something that looked like the fingers of a hand; a single hanging foot or animal pelt; dripping stalactites and mounting stalagmites. The blotches and splotches in the steel make for a kind of Rorschach test. Angles become abstractions; a weird Piranesian geometry incites vertigo. The woman who thought she was in a submarine was right.

And then there were the colors. Some of the surfaces looked like the drip paintings of Morris Louis or like fine-grained, well-sanded wood. Smudges and gradations relieved the steel's essential flatness, lending depth. When you go for the first time to the desert, in the American Southwest or elsewhere, you are overwhelmed by sameness. It's all *brown*. Then you look more closely and find the infinite variety of shades. Likewise, within the confines of Serra's steel, what looks like unvariegated rust opens up and reveals (I made a list) orange, ocher, brown, red, beige, tan, teak, rosewood, terra-cotta, black, white, yellow, pink, salmon, gold, mahogany, even gray. Every color from the rainbow except blue and green had its place or its moment.

As I paced through the Serra works, moving, stopping, and resuming, I experienced lines: the work, for all its three-dimensionality, had the flatness I prize in painting. I looked at a plane—vast, shaped, and curved, and more or less towering over me—and I saw color, texture, design, the hints or suggestions of pictures. I thought I was looking *at* a picture. We can adapt Klee's remark about taking a line out for a walk to Serra: now we take the walk through his walls and find the accidental lines on their surface.

Serra is the sculptor for the person who gets more pleasure from Cy Twombly's scripted or pseudo-scripted pictures, Jackson Pollock's swirls of color, and Richard Diebenkorn's geometrically arranged squares (as if Piet Mondrian had been redesigned by Henri Matisse) than from the blocks of Hans Hofmann, the monochromatic black-on-white of Franz Kline and Robert Motherwell, and the ferocity of much Willem de Kooning and Frank Stella. The art is quiet, and it inspires awe. It takes time to move through it and to allow it to move through you. Something so enormous and overwhelming has seldom seemed, when responded to correctly, so unthreatening.

Place and moment: space and time. The massiveness of the steel unveils shafts of color and hints of shape, suggesting rectilinearity and then refusing it in favor of curves. Because of counterweighting, the freestanding plates do not fall over, although they inspire vertigo and a vertical claustrophobia. The space remains constant, but it also changes as you go through it. As you move with the deliberateness of a tai chi exercise, you make a line through the walls and follow the trace of the lines on them. There is a path that you follow, and another that you discover. After a while you realize that you are experiencing, indeed performing, two different kinds of looking: noticing and observing. The first is random, spontaneous, and quick-eyed, requiring only the normal speed of a keen glance. The second is intentional and meditative. Seeing comes naturally; the eye darts. Looking comes with deliberation and composes the mind. Once activated, the mind settles into a paradoxical state of relaxed concentration—able to enumerate the colors, discover or invent the pictures on the walls—to focus on one thing and exclude others.

The essayist Linda Hall makes an appropriate, provocative distinction between two kinds of vision:

> Noticing is not observing. Observing is the hard stuff to which noticing may lead—noticing that gets out of hand, or, if you like, noticing that goes to one's head . . . Observation is an activity worthy of the metaphysician, who often acquires advanced degrees in it. Noticing is as pedestrian as it gets. There are jobs in noticing—busboy, bouncer, security guard, receptionist—but few careers.

Noticing is pedestrian; it's what we do when we are walking around, taking stuff in and registering the surround. It is seeing. The visible (James Joyce called it an "ineluctable modality": you can't get away from it unless you are literally blind) does not contain secrets; it does not contain inner depths. Everything is surface or appearance. And yet there is always something else to discover. Observing means you've got to stand still and wait, trying to save yourself by the act of looking.

4 Dancing

I had never thought that in middle age I would begin to learn something new, especially something physical. I had never thought that an obsession would be both so harmless and so easy to come by, immediate in its intensity and long-lasting in its pleasure. I had never thought that a single activity would begin in the body and extend through the mind and to the spirit. I had never thought that I could so easily be transported. And I had never fully appreciated, or applied to my own life, the truth of Willa Cather's observation in *My Ántonia*, subsequently carved onto her tombstone in Jaffrey Center, New Hampshire: "That is happiness; to be dissolved in something complete and great." In other words, I had never thought that I would become a dancer.

In retrospect I realize that the seed, although forgotten and dormant for decades, had been sown earlier. In my early teen years, when Philadelphia still held a place on the Broadway tryout circuit, I saw—in addition to serious dramas and comedies—many of the distinctive musicals of that much-maligned decade, the 1950s: *The Music Man, Greenwillow, My Fair Lady, West Side Story, Wildcat, Bells Are Ringing, Flower Drum Song,* and, most vivid in my memory, *Gypsy.* Like going to concerts at the Academy of Music (we sat in the highest part of the Amphitheatre), heading to Center City, as Philadelphians uniquely refer to their downtown, was part of middle-class culture. Our parents went at night; teenagers, like widows and senior citizens, went to Saturday matinees. Rock had only recently begun its inevitable push to overtake Tin Pan Alley and Broadway as the source of popular music, but musicals were still powerful—and musical—enough to plant themselves in our ears, and their tunes into what we whistled on the way to work or school.

At home, I had the only record player, a modest, portable "hi-fi" machine with tinny sound. Still, my parents knew the scores to the great stage hits from the thirties onward, most of which they had seen. I listened to LPs and 45s, and I sat at our upright piano pokily working my way through songs by Arlen, Berlin, Gershwin, Kern, Porter, Rodgers and Hammerstein, and, best of all to my incipiently sophisticated imagination, Rodgers and Hart. Whereas *The King and I* sounded soupy, lush, romantic, and full of goodwill (the very last thing a suburban teenager was interested in), *Pal Joey* was nasty, arch, and on the edge. I couldn't resist it, even before I learned that the version I played and heard had been stripped down, bowdlerized, sanitized, and stripped of Larry Hart's cynicism ("Until I could sleep where I shouldn't sleep," "Thank God I can feel oversexed again."). If this was what adulthood meant, I couldn't wait for it to start. At summer camp I had the good luck to be friends with the music counselor, who produced and directed watered-down versions of Broadway shows, and talent extravaganzas populated by distinctly untalented adolescents, and who actually knew all kinds of music, classical and popular.

When I fantasized infrequently about my own part in the Broadway musical of my mind, I never identified, as other gay boys did, with the female stars—Ethel Merman, Julie Andrews, Lucille Ball,

Judy Holliday, Carol Channing, and Roz Russell were objects of admiration but not emulation—nor did I ever think I had the stuff to be the leading man. Besides, it wasn't Curly I wanted to replace in *Oklahoma*, it was Will, and not only because of the name. Although I couldn't really sing, I enjoyed lip-synching my way along with Henry Higgins. But it was Stanley Holloway I wanted to be, not Rex Harrison. If only we had karaoke in those bygone days. In most shows, the second lead, whether *ingénu* or comic, always got the happy songs and the great dance numbers. Like Bill in *Kiss Me, Kate*, I preened, and then sang to myself the thoroughly silly "Bianca" ("I would gladly give up coffee for Sanka, / Even Sanka, Bianca, for you") before doing a pathetic tap number of my own devising. I entertained a certain fondness for the pajama-clad Yul Brynner and his polka with Deborah Kerr ("Shall We Dance?") in the film of *The King and I*, but what I really wanted to do was "Everything's Up to Date in Kansas City" from *Oklahoma!*, "Get Me to the Church on Time" (*My Fair Lady*), or "Big D" from *The Most Happy Fella*, because the zippy duet and the razzmatazz choreography were terrific and irresistible. I wanted to be—although I would not have said so at the time—a hoofer.

Dancers had fun. The South Philadelphia Italian teenagers on Dick Clark's *Bandstand* embodied sexuality, grace, and rhythm. Indeed, their grace and rhythm, even more than their slicked-back hair, their tight sweaters and pegged trousers, gave them their sexuality. We watched them on afternoon television when we came home from junior high school. They looked like creatures from some heroic world—the Land of Terpsichore?—far from the provinces of Acne, where we lived, only several miles but a virtual world away from them. They were stars. We were witnesses and wannabes. More nervous and bookish, we suburban adolescents tried to turn ourselves into these godlike urban idols at the Friday-night dances in the school gym. These South Philly kids didn't study dancing; they seemed to leap full-grown onto the stage, knowing all the right moves.

We, on the other hand, were undergoing the agony of cotillions, Saturday-afternoon dance classes conducted by severe, angular women who pressed a clicker called "the cricket" to call us to attention and to move us through our anxious paces: "*Slow, slow,* quick-quick" (the fox-trot); "Triple step, triple step, *rock step*" (the jitterbug); "*One,* two three; *one,* two, three" (the waltz); "Two, three, four and *one*" (the cha-cha). And so it went, inexorably. The girls stood a foot taller than the boys, and everyone had sweaty palms. For many thirteen-year-olds the payoff, the thrill, came in the form of one's first licit physical contact with another person. This particular rite of passage defined our coming of age as much as a bar mitzvah. Our parents told us that the lessons would prepare us for life. We didn't believe them. But they were right, and not only in reference to life at the country club. Good dancers make good neighbors, good citizens. It's not too strong to say that they are better human beings.

Then, in August 1960, Chubby Checker sang "The Twist," and dancing, of the sort I had grown up with, came to a halt. The individual now replaced the couple. The damage was not entirely irreparable, but a new chapter in our national cultural history had begun.

We flash forward more than three decades, past the sixties, the Beatles, and *Hair*; past hippies, pot, macramé, Be-Ins, heavy metal; past the disco seventies, Studio 54, the Bee Gees; past the eighties, Ronald Reagan and supply-side economics; past rap and hip-hop and techno and house. We move through world crises, oil embargos, the fall of Communism, and the reunification of Germany, as well as through countless changes in clothing, hair, makeup, and drugs.

In the mid-nineties a female friend, slightly battered and wearied from taking ballet class well beyond the age when it might have helped rather than hurt her middle-aged body, invited me as a guest to the ballroom studio where she was taking lessons. In an instant, the years fell away. I did not exactly feel that I had returned to junior high school, or that I was fourteen years old again, nor did I have any but the most vestigial muscle memory of the "steps." Instead, what I felt was instantaneous joy. The addiction had begun.

When asked "Why do you dance?" I am thrown back upon clichés and truisms. The primary goal is pleasure: will that suffice? Perhaps, but because I am an academic, wanting to know why is part of my intellectual wiring. The brain investigates the sources of, and reasons for, the pleasure of a repetitive activity that shares many qualities with—to name the most obvious analogies—sex, sport, and all the other creative and performing arts. Like any other label for a generalized sense of well-being, pleasure seems to interest existential and postmodern philosophers or theorists far less than gloom, despair, and neurosis, Kierkegaard's "fear and trembling," and Sartre's "nausea." Skeptical intellectuals all too often equate sanguinity with bovine contentment or repression; melancholy is mother's milk to them. (Go back to the Introduction.) But dancing or any activity like it provokes the kind of questioning that returns us to Aristotle and his *Nicomachean Ethics*. What comes first, an abstraction or its practice? A just man is recognized as such because he performs just deeds; at the same time, the doing of just deeds makes one a just man. At the start of chapter 9, Aristotle wonders "whether happiness is to be acquired by learning, habituation, or some other training, or whether it comes by virtue of some divine dispensation or even by chance." ("Wherein lies happiness?" asks Keats, in a different context.) Likewise, dancing either makes people happy or else it attracts happy people to begin with. Can we hope or imagine that a garden-variety depressive might waltz his way into cheerfulness?

Dance therapists can now routinely offer comfort as well as practical help to many ailing people. Members of the Mark Morris Dance Group give lessons to Parkinson's patients. Dance is a treatment for movement disorders, and patients find both joy in movement and a sense of community; they don't see what they are doing as simple therapy. Although the long-term benefits have not yet been calculated, the sessions increase the patients' confidence in their own balance. And even people without a debilitating disease can sometimes achieve near-miraculous change. At least one friend of mine claims that after taking up dancing she rid herself of a variety of mental and bodily ills. The moral: Put on your pumps, toss out your Prozac. How can we distinguish cause and effect; how can we know the dancer from the motivation for the dance?

Historically, dance has been connected to religious ceremonies—whether Apollonian and stately or Bacchic and ecstatic—and to social ritual, courtship, and the cementing of familial bonds. It marks, at least from the Renaissance onward, an affirmation of society's customs and of, above, all, the *politesse* that joins couples in marriage, then families, clans, and courts. Finally, it confirms the stability of an entire society. Dancing promises and celebrates cohesion. It is no wonder that Shakespeare's comedies and some of Ben Jonson's masques end with marriages and with the elegant movement of bodies to music as a symbol of conjoining. Nevertheless, such grand historical background information does little to explain the allure and the charm of dance to many of its contemporary participants. We are not taking part in stately or religious observances. We seldom don mythic costumes. Only first-time newlyweds, those bread-and-butter staples of Arthur Murray and Fred Astaire studios the world over, perform a planned choreographed routine at their nuptials.

Chaucer's five-times-married Wife of Bath calls the courting ritual "the olde daunce." Baldassare Castiglione lists dancing as one of the necessities for his perfect "courtier," whom we would call the Renaissance man. Jane Austen, that connoisseur of "the felicities of graceful motion," not only loved to dance herself but also used dancing as a motif throughout her fiction. Dance is an occasion, a means, a metaphor. "To be fond of dancing was a certain step towards falling in love," the narrator announces at the start of *Pride and Prejudice*. It is significant that Darcy at first refuses to dance with Elizabeth Bennet, or anyone else for that matter, and then that she is reluctant to dance with him. When they do dance, we know what's going to happen eventually. Darcy has a terse exchange with the tedious Mr. Lucas, who says, "There is nothing like dancing, after all. —I consider it as one of the first refinements of polished societies." To which our dour hero replies, "Certainly, Sir—and it has the advantage also of being in vogue amongst the less polished societies of the world. —Every savage can dance." But Mr. Darcy can't, at least not at this point in the novel. He won't dance; don't ask him.

Very much a figure of her age, Austen had to consider the delicate question of how much pleasure a respectable unmarried woman should derive from dancing. Total abandonment is never for her a desirable thing, or even a possibility, but dancing is a good and proper exercise (along with gardening and walking practically the only exercise for a young lady). It is a sanctioned form of erotic pleasure that has the additional, practical effect of preparing both woman and man for all future human negotiations.

Throughout her fiction, Austen uses dancing to test her characters' psychological, emotional, and social mettle. She acknowledges the strict rules of conduct that her original readers would have known but of which we are largely ignorant. An unengaged couple may not dance more than two dances in a row without raising eyebrows. (Charles Bingley violates the taboo and dances with Jane Bennet more than he should.) If a woman refuses one gentleman's invitation, as Elizabeth Bennet does that of Mr. Collins, she may not accept another partner. Darcy refuses to dance with anyone, since he claims that no woman attracts him, but it is incumbent upon a gentleman—notice how this rule still applies today—to ask an unpartnered lady to dance even if he doesn't want to. Darcy is rude. Society abhors a wallflower, as nature does a vacuum. A woman must not remain on the sidelines. In *Emma* Austen plants her tongue firmly in her cheek, and with equal wit and strength ironically reminds us of dancing's universal appeal and benevolent effects: "It may be possible to do without dancing, entirely. Instances have been known of young people passing many, many months successively, without being at any ball of any description, and no material injury accrue either to body or mind;—but when a beginning is made—when the felicities of rapid motion have once been, though slightly felt—it must be a very heavy set that does not ask for more."

In our century it is not novels but movies, with their larger-than-life figures on the screen, that make us most aware of dancing as a metaphor for desire. Even as an ancillary piece of the action, as in Hollywood comedies of the thirties with soigné couples in evening clothes sipping cocktails and smoking cigarettes before taking to the floor, ballroom dancing suggests the ease and desirability of upper-class life. More specifically, the dance represents the promise of the eventual sexual union of Fred and Ginger (in "Never Gonna Dance" from *Swing Time* they begin by refusing to dance but end up in fluid, elegant, graceful motion. We know what this means), or John Travolta and Olivia Newton-John (*Grease*), Patrick Swayze and Jennifer Grey (*Dirty Dancing*), or of any other couple in love. Dance may symbolize sex, or, in more polite terms, it may foreshadow it, especially for young people circling and cruising around one another, engaged in the hunt for a partner. In American popular culture of the past century, dance halls and ballrooms traditionally served as havens for forlorn people and the predators surrounding them. And then there are cruise ships, with round-the-clock dancing and an available staff that will make sure that no one has to sit any number out. All these venues supposedly attract sad sacks and solitaries of both genders. Think of Rodgers and Hart's tired ballroom hostess in "Ten Cents a Dance," who for "a dime a throw" gets porous stockings "with holes in the toes," as well as the ignominy of being manhandled by "pansies and rough guys, tough guys who tear my gown." No hero for her, just a "queer romance" and home to bed, alone.

Movies from the past two decades like Baz Luhrmann's *Strictly Ballroom* and Masayuki Suo's *Shall We Dance?* (remade as a much less persuasive American film starring Richard Gere and Jennifer Lopez) reinvigorate the old Hollywood tropes of dancing and loving. So does Al Pacino as a tango-dancing blind man in *Scent of a Woman*. For sheer sexuality, you can't beat the often garish displays afforded by professional ballroom competitions, brought to you on television, which feature outrageously lurid routines meant to titillate the crowd and the judges. And then, the latest unappetizing entry in the field of gladiatorial contests, television's *Dancing with the Stars* and *So You Think You Can Dance*. The scantily attired couples often look more like weird visitors from another planet than like real people we may meet on the street. They prance, they shimmy, and they writhe suggestively: it's no wonder that certain religious sects have traditionally prohibited even less immodest dancing.

In real-life ballrooms, however, the sexual rationale or angle may sometimes be necessary, but it is never sufficient, and often it is irrelevant. "What happens on the tango floor stays on the tango floor," says William Lawrence Parker III, describing Saturday-evening summer tango milongas in Central Park. The dancing couple—that frequent figure for the happiness of erotic union—can consist, for the three minutes of a single song, of two people who really do not know one another or, if they do, have no sexual interest at all in one another. George Bernard Shaw's witty aperçu—"Dancing is a perpendicular expression of a horizontal desire"—applies only some of the time. Apollonian ideals of restraint, decorum, and order may preempt Dionysian abandonment and inebriation. Social dancing confers, as well as derives from, dignity.

Health gurus promote dancing's cardiovascular benefits, but all the amateur dancers I know choose some other activity for mere exercise. Dancing satisfies a different need. Other people talk about "self-expression." They mean bodily release through energetic movement and the oblivion it produces. Such a release might come in the experience of solo disco dancing, or what happens at a rock concert where one is a separate, narcissistic part of a large mass of swaying people. It may also define more spiritual circumstances like those of dervishes whose stately flow builds to a whirling oneness with divinity. When dancing with a partner, however, you are or ought to be less self-involved than when dancing alone. You are also less absorbed in a union with the divine, because you are united with another human being whose abilities as well as needs may be quite different from your own. Neither sheer physical exertion nor the loss of the self in some larger entity suffices to justify the particular thrill of—say—a Viennese waltz that rotates and revolves, a slow bolero, or a fast, body-drenching salsa done to an earsplitting Cuban band.

At a certain point many dancers start hankering, even hungering, for competition, winning ribbons and medals. This is not an enterprise for the faint of heart or for anyone on a budget. Dance lessons and entry fees for competitions do not come cheap. But the practice and athletic discipline required to get in shape, and up to speed—to perform a sequence of maneuvers before sharp-eyed judges—hone one's physical and musical acuity. A potential Olympic sport, ballroom dancing demands split-second timing, judgment, artistry, and physical strength. There is nothing like working on routines with a professional or even an amateur partner to heighten the elegance and angularity of one's movements. People collect trophies for all kinds of activities—bowling, golf, and sports-car racing—so why not for dancing? For many amateurs, especially those with the necessary time and money at their disposal, the thrill of performance, even before a small audience of friends and relations, impels their energies, fans their dreams, and pumps their adrenal glands.

One acquaintance, a middle-aged schoolteacher of modest demeanor, told me that after her first scheduled three-minute performance with her instructor at our little dance club, the whoops and hollers of friends and relatives made her realize that she had finally found what she always craved and needed: applause. Seduced by the audience's love, she then got a cosmetic makeover and a personality transformation. Almost as an afterthought, she described a related thrill: the glamour of the costumes, the makeup, and the shoes. All women eventually come to realize that, for better as well as worse, shoes with high heels make for better dancers. They tighten the calf muscles; they push body weight forward. Every woman looks great in them, but they also, needless to say, eventually wreak havoc on the body. The professionals wear flats when teaching, reserving the heels for performance alone. The glamour does not come without an outlay. Feathers and furbelows take a big chunk out of a working girl's budget. Others may have such yearnings; I do not. Competitive activity never appealed to me. My Walter Mitty fantasies don't take this particular form. Team sports and the hullabaloo associated with fans, crowds screaming and yelling in violent ecstasy or moaning in inconsolable disappointment, all the pep of cheerleaders whipping a mob into a frenzy for the home team: again, not for me. In school I instinctively recoiled from anything en masse; groups of shrieking people egging on the heroes of the squad invariably suggested the Nuremberg rallies of the 1930s. Loud throngs—even those seen cheering at televised ballroom competitions—have always put me in mind of dangerously mechanized Fascist extravaganzas, and everything antithetical to polite, civilized life, to a society geared to the pleasure of an individual or of a couple. Again, Apollo, not Dionysus, is my god of choice.

Even though my first attraction to dancing came from a seat in the audience of musical shows, and although I sang and halfheartedly pictured myself onstage as the tap-dancing cowboy, the aging, buck and-winging vaudevillian, or the debonair, fox-trotting, top-hatted sophisticate, the thrill of performance before an audience held little appeal to the adult, social dancer I became. People require, and receive, applause in different ways. Since teaching demands a performer's instinct and talent, and elicits the gratitude of students for lessons learned or, more often, not learned, and for eye and mind-opening experiences in the classroom, my professional life has always massaged and assuaged my ego. It suffices. Finding myself in the spotlight in front of strangers or even friends watching me perform a choreographed routine (probably not too well) would be the least of my wishes. Instead, it would be my idea of torture. Losing myself in the activity, rather than finding myself, it has turned out, is what appeals to me. Dancing resembles looking, listening, swimming, reading: you disappear in doing it.

Neither self-expression, nor exhibition, nor exercise, nor courtship can explain the appeal of dancing to someone like me. Almost forty years ago, Irving Howe wrote a piece called "Ballet for the Man Who Enjoys Wallace Stevens" (*Harper's*, May 1971). The New York socialist intellectual amazed himself by the force of his response to George Balanchine's masterful choreography: "That an heroic leap or an elegant lift was exciting in itself could hardly explain the flood of pleasure, and sometimes the intensity of emotion, this dancing brought to me." And Howe was only looking, not doing. Balanchine's stated principle was to make the audience see the music and hear the patterns; his genius ensures that anyone who has ever watched *Symphony in C* will never again hear the score without picturing in the mind's eye his choreography. It is as if Bizet were waiting for Balanchine to come along a century later in order to complete his score. Something analogous happened to me—not as an audience member, but as an active participant—when I realized that the patterns one finds in poetry or music have equivalents in the figures one makes, often improvisatorily, along the line of dance. Both sides of the brain are fully engaged, especially when steering oneself and one's partner with batlike radar through the lines of traffic and having to make split-second decisions about what can and cannot be done in a crowd. You must plan and react quickly, in much the same way that you negotiate in a foreign language that you don't know very well. It's easy to arrange a sentence, or several of them, in advance of a conversation, but as soon as your interlocutor goes off in an unexpected direction, you must be able to revise your program without losing the thread of communication. Likewise, you might see a length of open floor space, perfect for weaving in and out of the zigzagging fox-trot step called the grapevine, only to have some other couple appear out of nowhere and cut off your lead. Time to rethink, although "think" is too ratiocinative a word; all deliberations must be made with quicksilver precision. The body does all the thinking.

Taking dance lessons—like trying to learn anything new after the age of twenty—challenges and humbles anyone, especially a person without a natural gift, and, even more, a person who himself makes a career of teaching. One becomes a child again. Again, the analogy to language acquisition obtains. The constant repetitive work of getting something into the memory, whether verb conjugations into the brain or steps into muscle memory, can baffle and tire, or even bore, the student. Wallace Stevens titled one poem "The Pleasures of Merely Circulating," and suggested in another that "merely going round is a final good . . . / The man-hero is . . . he that of repetition is most master" (*Notes Toward a Supreme Fiction*). He was not thinking pedagogically or athletically, but he might as well have been.

I once asked a very suave, magnetic young instructor how and when he got his start. Had he danced as a child or teenager? Oh no, he said; he had played sports in school. It turns out that, long before, he had had a girlfriend who dumped him. *Cherchez la femme!* When he asked her why, she said, perhaps grasping at straws, because he couldn't dance. Learning was his revenge. Not only did he learn to dance, but he also met his future wife at the studio. Now they own it. Dancing as a prelude to courtship does pay off for some. People find romance even when and where they do not expect to. How did he learn? "For the first few months I just stood in front of the mirror for hours at a time, moving forward and backward." Then, it was on to other things. If you can take the basic training without going mad or falling asleep, you are ready for more. Impatiently I once asked my dance teacher to teach me some *new* steps, but she sensibly replied, "Either I can teach you new steps *or* I can teach you how to dance." So I went back to Square One.

The basics have much to recommend them. Dancing has a lot in common with activities like tennis or chess. You always want to do it with someone at your level or above it, but you are often required to do it with someone not as good. One difference, of course, is that in dancing you are working with rather than against your partner. And although the steps are always the same, each partner is different, so one never finishes working on the simplest maneuvers. I have heard a story told of a golfer (whether true or not the tale is good) who every spring returns to his first teacher and importunes him: "Teach me to play golf." And they begin with the grip of the club, the addressing of the ball, the proper posture, the entire Zen sequence of preparation before any shot is attempted. This is an instructive anecdote in any case, but since, in my version of the myth, the golfer in question was Arnold Palmer, one realizes that even the best player or performer comes back, each time, to the very starting point of the activity, just as every painter or poet confronting the blank canvas or page must hope that he can move from the first gesture to the finished product. A tennis player spends hours hitting balls over a net before he meets a partner; a backyard hoopster shoots baskets without any teammates to help him. Doing the basics around the floor, over and over, not only builds confidence but also makes the elementary moves automatic by perfecting them. A glamorous woman, an excellent dancer, once asked me to dance with her at a party. I demurred, saying, "I'm not worthy to touch the hem of your ball gown." She laughed and said, "Listen, let me tell you a couple of things. First of all, any woman would rather dance with a rank beginner than not dance at all. Next, even if you know only two moves, I'm almost as happy to do only them as I would be to do the complicated stuff." What inspiring relief those words gave me. And off we went, I grateful for her sympathetic kindness, she happy to waltz in the least embellished way for the next three minutes.

As a teacher-turned-student, I feel not only instructed and humbled by my lessons but also made more aware of what my own students go through when I put them through their academic paces. I must remind myself: *they* are reading a poem for the first time, and I'm going round for the fortieth. Perhaps I need to back up or slow down. Every dance teacher has a different method, style, or technique for instruction. And each resorts to a different language, often figurative, to explain the physical phenomena that we do not understand except through the muscles or, if abstractly, through metaphors: "It's like holding a beach ball and having to turn your whole body to move it"; "It's like trying to walk in wet sand as you dig your feet down into it"; "It's like kicking a bit of dirt from the bottom of your shoe"; "It's like turning your wrist quickly to look at your watch"; "It's like having an imaginary wall between you, which neither of you can violate." So the instructions go. Natural dancers can watch a teacher do a step, indeed a whole sequence of them, and then perform a quick if imperfect imitation. They get it right, right away. The rest of us must go over the sequence until the mind has been numbed and we can do it with eyes shut or in our sleep. Practice makes, if not perfect, then at least possible.

As there are styles of instruction, so there are styles of learning. The naturals absorb through the eyes; the rest of us work through a combination of numbers and language. Once you know some elementary names—the five positions of the feet, underarm turn, forward rock, promenade, chassé—it's easier to go through the motions. If you can't count, you're liable to be in trouble. And not being able to hear the beat is probably the biggest impediment to success. At the start of my adult dancing life some friends invited me to join a gang from their studio (a single man is always welcome) for an evening's excursion to Rockefeller Center's old Rainbow Room, right before its unfortunate demise and then rebirth. I hesitated, but figured I should be a good sport. I told them I had three things to recommend me as a dancer: I liked dancing, I didn't mind making a fool of myself (this factor promotes good teaching as well), and I could hear the music's beat even if my footwork was not very fancy. Those who cannot follow the rhythms of the waltz had better stick to the jabs and thrusts of solo dancing in mosh pits. Enthusiasm counts for a lot, but it goes only so far.

One also learns in the classroom another basic law of dancing: the man leads, the woman or, as she is invariably called, the "lady" follows. Dancing may be the last arena for an old-fashioned sexism, although it also honors in part the phenomenon of "back-leading," which allows a woman in times of trouble to steer her partner over hazards in the line of dance in order to avert traffic collisions. Otherwise, all decisions fall for better or worse to the gentleman. Feminists might object. Activist Jill Ruckelshaus spoke with sincerity and with a large degree of psychological and political justification in a 1973 speech when she observed: "It occurred to me when I was thirteen, and wearing white gloves and Mary Janes and going to dancing school, that no one should have to dance backward all their lives [*sic*]." But her metaphor, although striking, was skewed. She misremembered the reality of dancing: the man *does* lead, and movement around the floor starts as he goes forward and his partner backward, but the woman decidedly does not "dance backward" most, let alone all, of the time. Male and female dance teachers learn both parts, and they all swear that learning to move backward is a picnic compared to the obligation of leading.

Such issues of power and control have other, often amusing, implications for any gender theorist. At the Gay Games in New York several years ago, a male-female couple was disqualified from participating in the ballroom competition. "But we are both gay," they replied. No matter: the management required *same-sex* couples, not necessarily gay people. In other words, dancing can blur rather than clarify issues of identity. The Round-Up Saloon, Dallas's most popular country-western dance hall, caters primarily to a gay male clientele, but everyone feels at home there. When the guys in their cowboy gear—ten-gallon hats, large buckled belts, jeans, fancy shirts with mother-of-pearl buttons, and tooled boots—start two-stepping or waltzing around the floor, simultaneously rotating and revolving, it is sometimes hard to tell who leads and who follows. And that's the point. Some dancers prefer one position exclusively, while others can play either part. Leader/Follower? Active/Passive? Butch/Femme? Top/Bottom? It's hard to know, and more important, it makes little difference when you are dancing. Twirling, two people become one.

It turns out that the quaint custom of the male lead, and its implications, are more widely acknowledged and accepted than one would expect in our post-feminist age. Once, at a party with some of my students, I listened to one young man lament his lack of success with women. The female students seemed curious and sympathetic, even amused. I said to the guy and to his female classmates, "Listen, kid, it's always nice or convenient to be handsome, rich, successful, powerful, intelligent, kind—and many other things as well—but if all else fails, if you learn to be a good dancer, it's very likely that some girl will love you." Most of the undergraduate women smilingly agreed. It is not just young people with raging hormones who subscribe to this idea. A sternly feminist colleague of mine said, when I mentioned that I was dancing, "Oh, I'd love to dance, but I need a really strong man to push me around." I told her, "Your secret is safe with me," but she had hit on an important detail: although pushing is strictly forbidden, a man who knows how to lead—with gentle power—can make any woman think that she knows what she is doing. The opposite is also true when the shoe, so to speak, is on the other foot: I never feel so polished and gifted as when dancing with a professional who can interpret my halfhearted, sometimes awkward gestures, and help me turn lurching stumbles into smooth glides. No matter who nominally leads or calls the shots, dancing is invariably a joint effort. It's your job, whoever you are and with whomever you dance, to make your partner, not yourself, look good.

One learns a great deal in other ways as well. Dancing teaches grace, a quality equally attractive in both men and women. "True ease in writing comes through art, not chance," wrote Pope in his *Essay on Criticism*, "As those move easiest who have learned to dance." Head up, shoulders down, the frame of the body solid and unbending, the arms strong but not overbearing, the space between the partners inviolate: that's the position to maintain and honor through all the movements. You can always identify a ballet dancer walking down the street by her distinctive body and turned-out feet. You can also pretty well identify a good ballroom dancer through the combination of his or her bearing, erect posture, and carriage. But carriage, like looks in general, can sometimes deceive. As with sex, you can glance at someone and say to yourself, "Man, I bet it would be fun to [dance or do something else] with [him or her.]" Don't count on it. Look around the hall. The ravishing, leggy, willowy blonde in the corner, that Grace Kelly double, might have a wobbly frame and spaghetti arms not strong enough to feel a lead. She may lack all sense of rhythm. Standing still, she's as pretty as a picture, but she's entirely dead once she starts to move. On the other hand, unprepossessing Ms. Short-and-Squat may feel like a feather and move with complete polish and assurance. Body weight has no relation to ease of movement. The guy done up like a Latin lover in his black muscle T-shirt? Once he takes the lady in his arms, all he can do is manhandle her, pushing and bulldozing his way across the floor, cutting off every other couple in his path like a juggernaut. Not a good dancer, no matter what he looks like. There, in the middle, notice the slightly stooped older gentleman, a seasoned dancer who husbands all his resources and knows how to move himself and his partner with the gentlest of signals. Dancing with him is as rich and delicious as butter. *Tango Argentina*, the great review that came to the States in the mid-1980s, featured middle-aged, well-fed, stocky dancers who looked like everyone's great aunts and uncles. That is, until they moved. Then you could see what years of training allowed them to do: stay absolutely rigid from the waist up, and sinuous and spidery from the waist down, as legs wrapped in and out of legs in positions you hardly thought possible for people who remained vertical. The best dancers combine strength and grace, steel and silk.

Such grace has its payoffs. As one improves, one manages to impress beginners or spectators by executing the most modest of moves with even relative success. Before a family wedding several years back, my cousins the mother and father of the bride had decided to take some lessons so as not to embarrass themselves on the floor. During an interval when the band had left for a break, and the recorded music played a Frank Sinatra fox-trot, I took to the center with my cousin Paula, and as we glided across the empty floor, twirling and pivoting and sashaying down the parquet, one of her old friends called out, "Paula, is that your dance teacher?" I took the question to mean that either you can fool some of the people some of the time or that my investment had reaped an incalculable dividend. At another recent wedding—of a college roommate—I had the feeling that grateful husbands were thrilled to relinquish their spouses to my care. "Take my wife, please," they might have said, but for the fact that the women themselves were lining up. Who knew how little it takes to be popular, if only for a few hours?

In the secular Western world that lacks the religious rituals of ancient Greece or of Eastern mysticism, dancing teaches another kind of grace, the most important of all: manners. Jane Austen knew what she was about. This grace forms the bedrock of a diverse society by encouraging, even requiring, civility. The dance teachers ("those brave ladies," as Donald Justice calls them in his tenderly reminiscent poem "Dance Lessons of the Thirties") who taught us to approach the girl—indeed, *every* girl—and say, "May I have this dance?" instructed us in the fine art of social generosity. Everyone remembers the drill: you extend your hand, you lead your partner to the floor, and afterward you return her to her place and thank her. And then you move on. In a place of social dancing it is every gentleman's responsibility to ask everyone, the worst—especially the worst—of the ladies as well as the best, to dance. Although I referred earlier to the somewhat reactionary sexism of the activity, we have at last, thankfully, arrived at a social point where women feel little compunction about asking a gentleman to dance with them. Neither male nor female should stay untended like a wallflower. Everyone asks everyone to dance. By courteously allowing everyone his or her place on the floor, you also have a working symbol for democracy. Making compromises on behalf of your partner, or tailoring yourself to someone else's abilities and needs, teaches lessons about tolerance that no civics class ever will. Manners mean accommodation to others. This is where I would rest my case for saying that dancers just may become better people than nondancers, as long as they carry these lessons with them from the dance hall. Dancing teaches awareness, deference, and kindness: what other activity does that?

And consider as well the very real consolation afforded by brevity. Unlike sports, a single dance takes relatively little time. Performing your social obligation and dancing with the rankest beginner or the clumsiest oaf will never last too long. Sometimes you may fear that you are riding a roller coaster to hell with a three-headed, three-legged moronic partner. Such is the grim fate of Dorothy Parker's unfortunate speaker in the deliciously mordant "The Waltz," who laments: "I hate this creature I'm chained to. I hated him the moment I saw his leering, bestial face. And here I've been locked in his noxious embrace for the thirty-five years this waltz has lasted. Is that orchestra never going to stop playing?" Of course it will, and the wounded and angry woman will go back to her floor-side table, slightly bruised and battered, but not really any the worse for a couple of shin kicks, and she will hope for something better in the next round. A good dance qualifies as a short romance; a bad one is easily forgotten.

Many writers—even men—have had kinder things to say about dancing than Parker. Wordsworth, the dourest of the British Romantics, recounts in *The Prelude* his memory of committing himself to poetry during summer vacation after dancing all night till dawn. "Wordsworth dancing" certainly sounds like an oxymoron, but the "din of instruments, and shuffling feet, / And glancing forms" precede "all the sweetness of a common dawn," in which his vocational dedication to work in the fields of poetry is made, unconsciously, for him. Frolicking in the fields before a major vocational decision: was this a mere coincidence or an issue of causality?

In a somewhat different vein, near the end of his life, Wordsworth's contemporary William Hazlitt wrote an essay for his ten-year-old son, "On the Conduct of Life; or Advice to a Schoolboy," that contains the following recommendation:

As to your studies and school-exercises, I wish you to learn Latin, French, and dancing. I would insist upon the last more particularly, both because it is more likely to be neglected, and because it is of the greatest consequence to your success in life. Every thing almost depends upon first impressions; and these depend (besides *person*, which is not in our power) upon two things: *dress* and *address*, which every one may command with proper attention.

If Hazlitt had known the tango, might he have eked out another decade? Probably not, but with his mature sense of "address," which lies within the individual's power, he encourages his son to observe matters of propriety and civility upon which personal "first impressions" and, following them, social intercourse depend. Psychologist Havelock Ellis went a step further in his *The Dance of Life*: "Dance is the loftiest, the most moving, the most beautiful of the arts, because it is no mere translation or abstraction from life; it is life itself."

Although it is often associated with narcissism or merely personal exhibitionism, dancing finally does allow escape and even transcendence. At the end of my happy evening at the Rainbow Room, I took my leave of the baker's dozen of amateurs with whom I had spent time. They were driving off to New Jersey; I was walking back uptown. It was New York in June, warm and promising. The hour was late, but Fifth Avenue was still filled with tourists, lovers, strollers, and dawdlers. I was happy, not drunk. Walter Mitty finally came alive in me. I have a visceral memory of swinging exuberantly around a lamppost (Gene Kelly, *Singin' in the Rain*), of flinging my jacket over my shoulder and loosening my tie (Frank Sinatra on the cover of one of his 1950s LPs), of executing pivots with an imaginary partner, an invisible Ginger to my inchoate, amateur Fred. "Maybe millions of people go by," "but I only [had] eyes" neither for her nor for myself but for the activity of which I had become simultaneously witness and performer. Any dancer can feel him- or herself turning into a version of Yeats's "body swayed to music," passive and active (the body "swaying" as well as "swayed"), both exerting will and power, and letting the self go. You adjust to the needs of a partner, and you also adjust to the demands of the song: by putting yourself at the service of another individual and of the accompanying music, you become an altered but heightened version of yourself. This isn't quite the same as saying that dancing makes you, ethically, a better person, or, psychologically, a more stable one, but it does make you happier, and part of that happiness comes from your dealings with other people.

The complete absorption of which Willa Cather wrote comes, in dancing, first through the attention to those details—of civility, posture, movement, traffic—that constitute the performance of the activity. Such concentration leads paradoxically to freedom, release, and a keener sense of grace. From rude beginnings and halting steps come lucidity and clarity. If dancing is self-expression, it is also self-denial. One loses the sense of individual personality, swept into and along with the music, indeed becoming a part of it. T. S. Eliot, strange as it may seem, loved to dance, both as a young man and late in life, when he'd married a second time—happily—after the failure of his first marriage. He had listening, not moving, to music in mind, but his epigrammatic wisdom pertains to one sensation as well as the other: "music heard so deeply / That it is not heard at all, but you are the music / While the music lasts" ("The Dry Salvages," *Four Quartets*). Ultimately, the pleasures of dancing promote an appreciation of, and a participation in, the life of art, specifically with regard to what Kant called its essential "purposefulness without purpose." Dancing lacks usefulness altogether. But it is not easy. In 1922 Heywood Broun allowed that "all there is to be said for work as opposed to dancing is that it is so much easier." We can talk about its benefits (cardiovascular, spiritual, social, psychological) and its symbolic or metaphorical analogues, but as the orchestra begins to play, we take to the floor yet once more for the purposes and joys (Stevens again) of "merely circulating." Years ago, at the Round-Up Saloon, I noticed a difference between the dancing cowboys and, by extension, any other dancing couples and the people I saw at discos: whereas the latter seemed to be grimacing, the former were always smiling.

I wrote on page 3 that this book had one of its beginnings with the fox-trot. This was at Lincoln Center's Midsummer Night Swing, where for three weeks every summer the plaza is transformed into a giant dance floor. You must pay to go in, but it costs nothing to stay on the concrete periphery and dance your heart out and the night away. I saw dancers of all sizes, ages, races, and abilities. Over the years Kitty Carlisle Hart, Robert Duvall, and Al Pacino have been spotted in the crowd. Who knows how many other celebrities have shown up incognito? Each evening begins with free lessons followed by one band, or several, often with a certain theme, style, or focus: West Coast swing one night, salsa another. People improvise together and help one another. Beginners learn patience and discipline; the more advanced improvise. A portly middle-aged man with a ponytail effortlessly tosses his partner over his head and between his legs, all the while keeping the beat. Stiff-looking Wall Street yuppies gradually unwind, loosening their ties and their hips. A veteran couple from Harlem ballrooms of a half century back swirls and twirls around as though time, but not their feet, has stopped. A Scarsdale fellow in Hawaiian shirt and Bermuda shorts boogies with his Talbots-clothed wife beside a zoot-suited Generation Xer with a pencil mustache and his chick in bobby sox and saddle shoes. Costumes or civilian clothes, it doesn't matter what you wear, just as long as you are there. Kids with body piercings and funky hair, who look as if they have never ventured north of Fourteenth Street, dance so well they make you think they've been doing it forever. I asked one such guy, a young sculptor-in-training whose outfit included suspenders and earrings (something old, something new), if this was true, and he said, "Oh no, just for three months."

Who's dancing? Everyone, that's who. Not just lovelorn widows, unhappy spinsters, shy computer geeks. Midsummer Night Swing is a miniature picture of democracy in action. Smiles are seen everywhere these summer nights on the plaza. On my way out, I stopped to have a word with a woman in a wheelchair—one of several I saw on the sidelines—who'd been tapping her hands and feet to the retro beat of Panama Francis and the Savoy Sultans. I asked whether she used to dance, and she said, "Of course." "Are you sad not to be able to do it now?" "Oh no. I loved dancing. Now I love watching. It's not as good as the real thing, but it sure beats everything else." She, too, had a smile on her face, delighted to be at the party.

More than fifty years ago, the philosopher Susanne K. Langer described "the ecstatic function" of dancing as the transport of dancers from a profane to a sacred state. She was thinking of dance as a religious rite; in our age, she went on, the transport moves from "reality" to "romance," what happens in a performance before an audience. But the audience, too, is transformed, and in its modest way can become a participant, like my wheelchair-bound senior citizen. Those who can, do; those who can't, bear witness and vicariously share the joy of movement. It's like people in nursing homes now confined to walkers and wheelchairs, and able to do only chair exercises, chair yoga. Where there is life there is—until the very end—at least modest mobility.

The fox-trot, like the waltz, the two-step, the polka, the swing, and all the others, has no raison d'être. There is no justification for it but one. I would like to understand Wallace Stevens's adverb—in the phrase "merely circulating"—quoted above neither in its modern, deprecating sense nor in any other ironic one, but in its etymological truth: "mere" means "pure," "undiluted," "perfect." Likewise, dancing again and again around the floor produces the human feeling that partakes of the essential and the ornamental in equal measure, what Wordsworth, in the preface to *Lyrical Ballads*, labeled the "grand elementary principle . . . that constitutes the naked and native dignity of man": *pleasure*, pure and simple. Pursuing such pleasure one is also pursued and overcome by happiness.

5 Listening

A lthough this essay concerns music, it opens with a search for silence.

On September 12, 2001, in the aftermath of the previous day's tragedy, the voices began in earnest: not only those of journalists, commentators, and news analysts, whose essential reports we had awaited, clung to, and hovered over for twenty-four hours, but also those of preachers, politicians, and assorted pietymongers. Never did the inadequacy of language seem more striking, or the noxious stridencies of the human voice more grating. Never did silence sound more welcome, consoling, even necessary. I suppose that some of my fellow citizens took comfort in hearing their government officials and clergymen shake fists, vow vengeance, and invoke the deity. I, however, did not want words, from either well-meaning hacks or self-righteous avengers. The only words that seemed to me wise and meaningful on September 11 and afterward were those from William Butler Yeats's 1938 poem "Lapis Lazuli": "All things fall and are built again, / And those that build them again are gay." Looking back two decades to one set of disasters and looking forward to another one already on the European horizon, Yeats does not grieve, nor does he explain why horrible things happen. They just happen. His poem hardly offers the judicious or hopeful combination of solace and retaliation that may appeal to an angry and mourning audience; rather, it articulates the cold, true facts of history.

When speech was meaningless, music offered some comfort, but most of all I wanted quiet. So I went to church, an unconventional church appropriate for an unconventional person.

Those of us whose material is language are aware of what it can and cannot do. In times of trouble, how and where do we find our consolation? Even a religious Refusenik like me has been known to enter places of worship, often for a wedding or a funeral, sometimes for the aesthetic pleasure of artistic performances, and once in a great while out of a need to test the waters of what goes by the name of spirituality. Like Philip Larkin, whose "Church Going" describes stopping by a country house of worship out of a combination of incredulity and wonder, and like countless other undoctrinal nonbelievers, I sometimes find myself drawn in. Larkin ends his poem:

> *A serious house on serious earth it is,*
> *In whose blent air all our compulsions meet,*
> *Are recognised, and robed as destinies.*
> *And that much never can be obsolete,*
> *Since someone will forever be surprising*
> *A hunger in himself to be more serious,*
> *And gravitating with it to this ground,*
> *Which, he once heard, was proper to grow wise in,*
> *If only that so many dead lie round.*

The human hunger for seriousness, an innate compulsion to find wisdom and authority, makes us gravitate, that is, move downward, to buildings whose spires reach upward. We have hopes along with doubts. Even the atheist, and especially the agnostic, can look longingly at religion's structures, both its buildings and its ideologies, with envy, nostalgia, and also disbelief. In "High Windows," another poem that reckons with faith, Larkin acknowledges the historical and cultural decline of religious authority, the iron grip of the Anglican establishment, and then he turns his attention upward, to and through the church windows that obliterate language. They remind us of the great beyond of human aspiration and simultaneously of the unlikelihood of salvation:

> *Rather than words comes the thought of high windows:*
> *The sun-comprehending glass,*
> *And beyond it, the deep blue air, that shows*
> *Nothing, and is nowhere, and is endless.*

Within the empty country chapel of "Church Going," Larkin heard silence. Now, thinking about "high windows," he again moves from words to silence, from society to heaven. Ultimately "comprehending" nothing other than human doubt and our individual need to overturn it, Larkin arrives at no solid conclusion. He doubts, he seeks; he acknowledges the endlessness and the nothingness of the deep blue air, which we look at, always from a distance, with wistfulness.

Wistful, wondering, and doubting, like Larkin, I sought silence and community the Sunday after the disaster at a Quaker meeting, a form of worship I knew about from Philadelphia, my hometown, as well as from Boston and even from Dallas, where a small branch of the Society of Friends manages to hold itself together in the land of guns, in a state that loves the death penalty. What George Fox's Friends perfected more than three centuries ago still exercises a profound appeal to antihierarchical, antiestablishment Christians and agnostics alike. The simplicity of the Quaker creed—that the inner light shines within all of us, and therefore that all human life is sacred—goes against the mysteries of Christian transubstantiation, against pomp and liturgy. Sitting still and quiet on a hard-backed bench for an hour has brought me as close to a religious experience as I am likely to come. I measure the success of Quaker meetings inversely to the amount of time I must listen to others speak. Silence is best; speech is intrusive. One should speak only when moved to do so by that inner spirit. "Speech after long silence," said Yeats in a different context.

Because Quakers are instructed in the art of brevity and are admonished not to use the meeting as a platform or a soapbox, they usually speak softly, tentatively, and to the point. As part of the meeting, one is constrained to listen for the truth, just as one is obliged to look for the inner light in all people, even or especially those who appear least likely to embody it. Think of it in terms of other professional activities. Consider the way a psychoanalyst is trained to go within his patient's words to hear the meanings underneath, to bring up to consciousness what is not being said. A teacher, too, must listen to what his students say. A reader of a poem listens for its tone, the meanings beneath the meanings. Listening requires, above all else, endurance.

I once asked the distinguished American pianist Richard Goode who his most important teacher was. "Mieczyslaw Horszowski," he replied unhesitatingly, referring to the old master who died one month short of his 101st birthday in 1993 but was still performing and teaching until almost the very end. Goode had studied with him as a younger man at the Curtis Institute, and then returned for the occasional tune-up, checkup, or coaching session. "What did he say to you that was useful?" I wondered. "It's not that he said anything in particular," Goode replied, "but he *listened very carefully.*" The master's sheer concentration communicated some deep truths or tricks of the trade to the ever responsive, now adult student.

On those first two Sundays following the attacks, I sat in simple silence, and when others spoke, I attended to their words. I tried to listen very carefully. Mostly I closed my eyes and felt my blood pressure go down. At the end of the hour, when the day's leader turned to her neighbor and said "Good morning," initiating a round of "Good morning"s throughout the assembly, I resumed normal, daily, secular life. People ask me why I want to drive to a silent meeting instead of sitting quietly at home and meditating, Buddhist-style, on my own mat. I tell them that there is power as well as comfort in being surrounded by other people, many of whom are like-minded, gentle pacifists. One cherishes a community, even in silence, because a silent group speaks volumes.

As with silence, so with sound: sometimes solitude is the best society, and sometimes you want to share a heard experience with others. The literary and musical scholar Lawrence Kramer has said that after 9/11 he could not be alone with his CDs, that he took solace from music only in the company of other people. Sadness likes company; listening with someone else enlivens an auditory experience.

Music—more than other kinds of sound, especially language—often permits us to hear, and to listen to, the deepest wellsprings of knowledge. Music grants entry to what Wordsworth called "thoughts that do often lie too deep for tears," by which he also meant too deep for words. For a secular person, music gives the closest access to transcendence that he is ever likely to have. When Walter Pater said that "all art continually aspires to the condition of music," he meant quite simply that all art wants to reach that place—deeper or higher than the place of the politicians and preachers of 9/11—which moves past language's capacity to deceive and confuse. And when Goethe called architecture "frozen music," he meant that pure form, whether in time or space, has certain meanings and forms of feelings that exist beyond our capacity to name them.

After a year had passed, after the babble of sermons and speeches, a memorial was held at Ground Zero. For me and others, the most moving part of the service was also the simplest, the point at which words were used only as labels: the recitation of the names of the dead from A to Z. These were words without commentary, analysis, and ornament; they were words beyond human emotion. And they said all that could be said: here are the people, the victims, a United Nations of the dead. The simplest tribute was the least pretentious, the least striving after explanation or revenge. It was the tribute that came closest to the condition of music, in the same way that the modest capsule biographies published over the course of months in *The*

New York Times under the neutral heading "Portraits of Grief" captured far better than funerary tributes the glorious ordinariness of the day's victims. No embellishment, just an anecdote or two, often banal, and therefore always tear-provoking. The sheer impersonality of the recitation made for a greater depth of feeling than any fancier articulation that might offend our aesthetic sensibilities. Because so few people know how to produce genuine eloquence, it's always better to stick to a plain and simple script.

Mostly, in the days following the September 11 attacks, I turned off the TV and radio, I blotted out the talking heads, and I listened to music: late Beethoven string quartets, Bach preludes and fugues, Mozart piano concertos, Handel concerti grossi. Some decades before, on the weekend of November 22, 1963, my college roommates and I played masses and requiems—by Bach, Mozart, Beethoven, Brahms, Verdi, Fauré, and Stravinsky—and sat in silence and tears thinking of President Kennedy and the events in Dallas and Washington. All these compositions, whether with or without words, are emblems and forces of order, balance, and concentration. They exist in the listener's ears totally independent of the human will to power. Composed by living human beings, the requiems and funeral masses especially embody a truth once articulated by George Bernard Shaw in response to the great arias of Sarastro in Mozart's *The Magic Flute*: "The only music yet written that would not sound out of place in the mouth of God." They give evidence of divine power.

Musical conventions vary from culture to culture. A Westerner cannot understand the scales and harmonies of Eastern music without exposure, practice, and study. But music has supposedly universal charms. It holds special ones for people who live most consciously, obsessively, in and with language. After the more primal senses of touch and smell, sound comes to us as infants well before sight does. Babies in neonatal nurseries can recognize early on, even from a distance, the particularities of maternal billings and cooings—their distinctive pitch and tone if not their words—and they can distinguish their native language from those of the other kids. Not for nothing do we say "mother tongue" or "*mame loshn*." Sound connects us to nurturing, to fathers as well as mothers, to divinity. God created the world with a command ("Let there be light") and the Gospel of John reminds us of the *logos*, the word: "In the beginning was the word, and the word was with God, and the word was God." In Judeo-Christian mythology, at the Last Judgment noise will overwhelm the cosmos and time will end. As the last trumpet sounds, and the dead are raised incorruptible, the saved will be resurrected, the lost will be damned, and in the words of John Dryden, which Handel set in his "Ode to Saint Cecilia," "music shall untune the sky."

Here is my oldest memory, or so I think: I am sitting on my mother's lap and being sung to. And I remember the songs. They set my musical tastes then and there. They included nothing contemporary and nothing from my mother's girlhood; instead, she sang the songs of *her* mother's day, songs from the turn of the last century. These were the songs my mother taught me, and they were also the ones her mother had taught her. Sentimental parlor ballads ("She's Only a Bird in a Gilded Cage"); gentle lullabies ("On the Banks of the Wabash Far Away"—we lived nowhere near Indiana nor had anyone in the family ever seen it); rousing and tender stuff by George M. Cohan and Irving Berlin ("Mary's a Grand Old Name," "Always"). It was no wonder I grew up attached to a long-distant past and with a fondness for sentiment and treacle, *Schlag* and *Schmaltz*. Anything in three-quarter time, any waltz, any 32-bar AABA old classic will bring a tear to my eye. Ditto "Alexander's Ragtime Band," grandstanding and ebullient, reminiscent of band concerts in the park, gentlemen in straw boaters, ladies with parasols, the set of an MGM musical from a simpler world that existed only in our collective imagination. A world of major keys, and of dominant seventh chords always resolved. The pastoral world of operetta, whether American as apple pie (Victor Herbert) or Austrian as Dobosch-torte (Franz Lehár's *The Merry Widow*). I am still a sucker for all of it. "Meet Me in St. Louis"? You bet.

Music in our house came from three sources, which often overlapped: my mother's enthusiastic, off-pitch voice, which I inherited; her slightly more proficient piano playing, which I also picked up; and the radio. Years before I bought the family's first "record player" or, as we called it, "hi-fi," a portable thing in its own leather case which I toted off to college with me, we heard Kate Smith sing "God Bless America" and "When the Moon Comes Over the Mountain," songs she repeated once she transferred her show to television. Many wonderful things happened to those of us who grew up before TV. One—as I describe it in chapter 1—is that we became readers. Another is that we became listeners rather than lookers. We heard the human voice, and we heard disembodied notes coming from a wooden box or a car radio. We pricked up our ears and we received sounds unaided by our eyes. I was born to become a listener.

To this day, I listen with my eyes closed, not just to music, but also to words. A while back, Garrison Keillor brought *A Prairie Home Companion* to Dallas. I'd been a fan for two decades, ever since the late James Merrill, the most mandarin of postwar American poets, introduced me to the program. A more unlikely pair I couldn't imagine: the deep-voiced populist weaving the tales of Lake Wobegon and its cast of more-than-ordinary characters, and the patrician aesthete, world traveler, and connoisseur of subtlety. But I came to see, or hear, what Merrill heard in Keillor: it was all in the voice. He was a storyteller who relied on tone, and tone, the sine qua non of poetry, the essential measure of emotional temperature, is another word for manners. Merrill seemed to be all artifice, Keillor all nature, but it was only an apparent dichotomy that separated them. They were twin sides of one coin, the fancy and the plain, the urban and the rural, the voices of the metropolis or the cosmos itself and the voice of the small town. They both created magic through voice, whether spoken or transcribed onto the page. It turns out that the cosmos is just the small town writ large. The human voice: it's the organ of comfort and provocation, assurance and anxiety. Merrill and Keillor and all the others are just storytellers around a campfire, late at night, darkness covering their faces.

Friends asked whether I wanted to go to the live performance of *A Prairie Home Companion.* Tempted for a moment, I came to my senses and realized that I didn't want to see, to watch, to become a modest part of the genial audience that participates audibly and necessarily each week. Keillor himself has said that radio is the line of work for someone who's not good-looking; for a radio job you don't even have to dress, or look, your best, in order to have the right effect. My Saturday-evening listening pleasure comes—whenever I have the liberty—from making a drink, turning off the phone, and sitting quietly in a chair, watching the sun begin its decline into twilight, and then shutting my eyes. I open my ears and the magic begins. Why would I want to spoil the sound effects by seeing them made? Do you really want to know how the magician saws the lady in half? I never did. Out of sight is not out of mind, but rather the opposite: a soothing voice gives comfort as well as stimulation.

From the age of ten until I left home for college seven years later, I had on the headboard of my bed a small AM–FM radio. After reading, after turning off the light, I would listen in darkness while waiting to fall asleep. Once out, I might linger in semiconsciousness, hearing faintly the sounds from the box before finally and unknowingly flicking off the switch. On the rare days when I was home from elementary school, sick but not so sick as to lie unconscious, I could hear the voices of afternoon radio shows, serials and soaps, talk and music, *The Lone Ranger* and *Stella Dallas* and the local news stations. A couple of years later, if the cloud cover was just right, I might get country-western music from WWVA in Wheeling, West Virginia, worlds away. Or, both physically closer but culturally much farther, on Sunday nights I could listen to Jean Shepherd, the first real audio "performance artist" before the phrase was known, recite his jazz-inflected monologues on WOR from not-so-distant Manhattan. He might as well have been speaking from Mars instead of ninety miles to the north, from a place where people stayed up late and smoked and drank, where hip cats who played bongo drums, and wore berets and shades, went with their chicks to Fifty-second Street for jazz or to the Village for Beat poetry in coffeehouses. I could hear sophistication, so near and yet so far, and I longed to have it.

During the golden age of American popular music, the three decades plus from the end of World War I through the proliferation of television in the land, radio was the medium not only of communication and togetherness—families sitting around of an evening listening to Jack Benny and Fibber McGee and Molly—but also of intimacy. The medium, not the composer, made music happen. Irving Berlin and George M. Cohan got their start on Broadway, but as the composer Cy Coleman said, when he was a kid: "It never occurred to me that the songs were written by different people. They were just The Radio." When MTV videos took over, a different aesthetic developed. Everything was in your face, as well as in the faces of the performers, who did more than merely sing. But Bing Crosby and Frank Sinatra caressed the microphone, and they sounded better on the radio, and later on records, than in person. They didn't have to raise their voice, and they worked quietly to produce their own sound.

Best of all, the listener could believe that he or she alone was being sung to. Just as a book speaks to one reader, a singer addresses a single listener. And then the listener might sing along. It's long been noted that Crosby was as popular with men as with women, because every American man thought, singing to himself in the shower, that he sounded just like the famous crooner. On the radio everything sounded like a cabaret. Mabel Mercer, who Sinatra said taught him all he knew about how to deliver a song, was in many ways the greatest pop singer of her age. We have no recordings from her early career in Paris, during the thirties and forties. The records from the fifties give us her voice on the wane, but you can still hear her speaking, or caressing, those lyrics. Soft voices, safe places: a singer on the radio inspired a sense of belonging.

Even before my teen years, when I made a vicarious escape

through listening to the radio, I sat, like Eudora Welty, listening to the grown-ups talk. Storytellers all begin as great listeners. We think of stories and storytelling as the province of Southerners like the young James Agee, falling asleep in Knoxville in the summer of 1915 (the passage from *A Death in the Family* beautifully re-created by Samuel Barber's setting for soprano and orchestra). Or like Welty herself, who credited her storyteller's instincts to her gene pool. People who listen carefully may become people who talk, or write, well themselves. Any child born with his ears open has a similar story. I listened to the adults, my grandparents and their siblings, my parents and theirs, on warm Philadelphia summer weekend afternoons, sprawled on chairs and sofas sipping iced tea, lemonade, and ginger ale, taking in radio broadcasts of Phillies' games. They paid attention, which then wavered; they made small talk; they took naps. The lazy afternoons flowed gently in and out of consciousness.

Always there was the talk, overheard as well as shared, the kind of talk that Elizabeth Bishop describes in her late poem "The Moose," about a nighttime bus ride from Nova Scotia to Boston, during which she dreamily eavesdrops on the faint conversations in "a gentle, auditory, / slow hallucination" behind her:

> *In the creakings and noises,*
> *an old conversation*
> *—not concerning us,*
> *but recognizable, somewhere,*
> *back in the bus . . .*

What are they talking about, "uninterruptedly . . . in Eternity"? The stuff of ordinary life: what he said, what she said, who died, who married, who went crazy, who went bad. And always with faint sounds of acceptance and understanding, never of surprise or incredulity. Even tragedy, when woven into the fabric of ordinary life, becomes domesticated. Think of the idiom: we "take it all in." Listening, we internalize life and vicariously live it. Listening, whether to parents at bedtime, relatives in the parlor, or strangers on the bus, satisfies a craving for stories, for intimacies.

Music, too, has intimacies, the first ones shared by the singing parent and the listening child, later ones communicated between performer and audience, or between long-playing record, disc, or tape, and listener at home or with headset, iPod, or car radio. At nine I borrowed a clarinet from the elementary school storeroom and began lessons. A year later I switched to piano. By chance, or perverse choice, I managed to do things backward: instead of starting with classical music, scales, exercises, and modest theory, I began taking lessons in pop music with my mother's piano teacher, one of a pair of amiable young men who enhanced their modest salaries as junior high school teachers by driving in the afternoons and early evenings through our neighborhood and offering instruction to the gifted and not-so-gifted children of middle-class families. Some were playing under duress. Others, like me, with or without talent, actually enjoyed playing. Living in a small house with the sounds of any child other than a prodigy playing an instrument testifies to a parent's love, masochism, or sadism. My younger brothers went for the clarinet and the trombone, respectively; I guess our parents were grateful as well as lucky that no one pressed for percussion, and we were all still too early for the electric guitar.

I was trained to cheat. I played popular music, some of it on brittle yellowed sheets that my mother had used when she was a teenager two decades before. I could read the treble line, but instead of learning the bass clef, I resorted to the guitar chords written above the stave. My two teachers made late-night money by playing in unglamorous cocktail bars like the one at the local Howard Johnson's restaurant. I was on track to join them, tickling the ivories for the listening pleasure of soused suburban lounge lizards: it turned out that I could read well, keep the beat, and I had almost perfect pitch. I supplemented my seventh-grade renditions of classics from a quarter century back, "Don't Blame Me," "Smoke Gets in Your Eyes," with hipper stuff like the Everly Brothers. Luckily I switched, two years later, to more serious chores with a real musician, who put me through my awkward paces all throughout high school. Then, woosh! In no time flat I was on to Mozart sonatas, Chopin mazurkas, and Bach two-part inventions. I played none of them well, and never endured the agony of performing in an annual school recital, but something in my lessons took hold. For every false note and inept arpeggio I played, I have listened more intently and with greater appreciation to those who do it better. And I learned to sit still: like attending Quaker meetings, piano playing enforces good posture upon a young person, even when you don't have a hectoring instructor who beats your hands with a ruler and gets you to maintain a rigid pose. Some things just happen by themselves.

By the time I could wander around Center City Philadelphia, haunting Leary's bookstore, developing a taste for urban walks down eighteenth- and nineteenth-century streets lined with stately row houses and brownstones and shaded by gingko and locust trees, I also started hanging around record stores. Well before they all went out of business, the serious music stores stocked sheet music and records and—in a throwback to the forties—one or two would still allow you to take a record into a listening booth to try it out. The Big Time hit Philadelphia when New York's Sam Goody opened a retail store on Chestnut Street. Classical LPs went for about $2.50 when I was in high school, and frequent sales brought prices down still further. When I was fifteen, I bought my first records, Guiomar Novaes playing the first book of Debussy *Préludes* and Szymon Goldberg doing the Brandenburg Concertos. Records had beautiful covers, along with legible jacket copy and informative booklets. Compared to the beneficent manufacturers of classical LPs, the man who invented the packaging and print for compact discs was a sadist.

We supplemented home listening with concertgoing. The Academy of Music, the Philadelphia Orchestra's venerable nineteenth-century hall, hosted Saturday-morning children's concerts, less dramatic versions of what Leonard Bernstein was doing on television and in New York. They were the bane of most suburban kids, because they required proper clothing, dresses and Mary Janes for girls and, for us boys, coats, ties, and itchy flannel trousers. In spite of our scratching, fussing, and yawning, in spite of narrow, uncomfortable seats, something took; six years after being dragged by dutiful mothers, we came back by ourselves, usually buying rush seats in the Amphitheatre (with its own entrance) for fifty or seventy-five cents, running up five flights to claim our places in the Gods, and leaning over to see imperious Eugene Ormandy put his finely oiled machine through its paces. Once a year Leopold Stokowski came to town, using the magical hands that Disney glamorized in *Fantasia* to charm both his former players and his Philadelphia fans. From the top you could see everything, although in miniature. And you had the feeling of surround sound as well as the hominess of being in the company of like-minded music lovers. In October 1960, on his first American tour, Sviatoslav Richter walked onto the stage, sat down, and played the Brahms Second Piano Concerto, and after the thunderous applause did something I have never witnessed since: he encored the final movement. It was the stuff of legend.

As I grew, I expanded my musical as well as other horizons. From an early love of musical comedy I moved to Gilbert and Sullivan in high school. Who could resist the combination of farce and sentiment, of lush and jaunty tunes and witty, arch, sometimes mind-bending lyrics? "Turbot is ambitious brill"? I wondered for days about that one, before consulting the dictionary. And who were all these people, the proper names strewn throughout the lyrics? "The science of Julien, the eminent musico– / Wit of Macaulay, who wrote of Queen Anne– / The pathos of Paddy, as rendered by Boucicault– / Style of the Bishop of Sodor and Mann." Starchy military bluster wrapped around lists of names and set to a tune immediately memorable, hummable, singable. I was getting a course in British history and nineteenth-century culture, although those lessons came as an afterthought, a lagniappe. I hungered for pleasure, and knowledge came unsought. I convinced myself, or at least pretended, that I could sing almost as well as Martyn Green. I spent hours memorizing and repeating all the lyrics to the patter songs, my ear to the record player and my eye to the libretto or the score. (I learned from a helpful librarian that I could borrow an entire orchestral transcription.)

By college I had moved on to opera, first on records (Anna Moffo, Robert Merrill, and Richard Tucker in *Traviata*, Eberhard Wächter and Graziella Sciutti in *Don Giovanni*), then live. Leontyne Price as *Aida* at the old Met in my sophomore year: from the rafters, nothing was quite visible, but the sound poured out and forth, and Price pitched her high notes—the soft as well as the loud ones—up to us in the heavens.

About opera, I am not a crazy person. I don't scream "Brava, diva!" and go berserk. I never worshipped at the feet of Callas, Tebaldi, or Sutherland. What I wanted was music, pure if not simple, and to this day, if a performance is weak, I can imagine in my mind's ear or eye what it might be. If the tenor doesn't hit the high note dead center, he hasn't entirely spoiled my evening. Some singers are not as engaging as others, and even the good ones have off nights: would I want to stay home with perfect recordings and never venture into the house and risk a live performance? Well, that's what many fans do after a certain point. It's like what pianist Glenn Gould finally took to, preferring to control the mechanics and reproduction of his sound in the recording studio rather than confront a live audience and risk spontaneity while playing.

Still, hope springs eternal. One lives for the authentic shock that comes only when everything and everyone function at full strength. It seldom happens, especially in the age of weird operatic updating, dramatic *mises-en-scène* with shock appeal but no dramatic rationality. In those cases it's easy to ignore what is happening onstage and focus on the voice. Shutting the eyes often helps. If the voices in a live performance do not seem especially good, you can concentrate on the music itself, the Platonic voice or singer you wish to hear in the role. This is what many professional musicians and musicologists do, and they are usually much less interested in the physicality of the production than in its musical qualities. The critic John Ardoin once said to me that he'd just come back from a mediocre performance of Bellini's *Norma* ("my favorite opera") at the Fenice opera house in Venice ("my favorite opera house"), and he added, "If Veronica Nobody had been singing the title role, I'd still go." That's what we call a *music* lover.

At a recent college reunion I spoke, along with a classmate, to a group about our interests in opera. He went first. I realized from the title of his talk, which included the word "demented," that he was going to speak on behalf of the Dionysian side of music. Me? Apollonian all the way. It is the voices and the music that count for me, seldom the staging, even less the offstage, real-life shenanigans of the stars. In today's visually obsessed culture, it is not an exaggeration to say that great singers may soon be pushed offstage by better-looking youngsters with toned bodies and occasionally amplified voices. Good to look at, but can they sing? Several years ago a producer did *La Bohème* on Broadway, with a young cast who might have just come from *Rent*, the updated version of Puccini's story of young starving artists. He was hoping to interest the audience of *Rent* in the original version. I went to a matinee, and to wash the bad sounds out of my ears I had to go to the Met that evening to hear real singing. The kids looked fine, but they were not—at least not yet—opera singers.

Wagner wanted a *Gesamtkunstwerk*, an opera in which everything worked together, and he controlled every aspect of his productions. How seldom, these days, does a production intelligently complement and support, rather than interfere with or undermine, the music and the drama. I can count on the fingers of one hand the number of operatic productions whose "visuals," as we now call them, I still remember. The most impressive was the simplest: John Dexter's inexpensive (there was a budget crunch) 1976 production of Poulenc's *Dialogues of the Carmelites* at the Met, performed on a mostly bare stage and opening with the nuns in their habits splayed facedown on the raked floor in the form of a cross. The opera ends with an ascent to the scaffold as the huddled, soon-to-be-martyred women sing their final prayer to the Virgin and march singly to an invisible guillotine that slices off each head with a whoosh. The voices are gradually diminished. At last, there are none.

Total silence, an audience's most powerful response, followed, rather than the applause and shouts that characteristically begin before the final chord or the falling of the curtain, and before the now ubiquitous standing ovation. On the subject of applause, here's what Hugo Wolf said in 1885: "Why in the name of heaven and all its angels must the searching fire of enthusiasm always come out through hands and feet? Why must there be clapping and stamping? Do the public's hands and feet constitute the movable lightning rod for the electrified soul? I ask whether applauding is allowable under all circumstances, whether it is a force of nature—or only a bad, a stupid habit." At its best, music should inspire stasis, not a simultaneous uproar and a rush for the exits.

In my sophomore year at college, I heard Don Giovanni try to seduce Zerlina with "*Là ci darem la mano*," on records. The same sublime Mozartian delicacy had moved me the year before, when I listened to my first Mozart piano concertos. A classmate was making spare change by selling LPs door to door. I bought Robert Casadesus playing the eighteenth and twentieth concertos, and my musical life changed in an auditory flash. The dark first movement of the D minor concerto (#20), followed by the elegant simplicity of the second movement and the conclusive synthesis of the third, taught me something about the relationship between passion and restraint, the regulation as well as the production of feeling, and the uses of repetition. It taught me about balance, development, and synthesis, about tension and resolution. So did the arias from *Don Giovanni*. Anyone who is listening would be seduced by the Don's apparently sincere invitation to the peasant girl. That's what music does. And in these cases, not knowing Italian can work to your advantage, because the music taken without the words articulates forms and feelings that language cannot set forth. Music cannot lie. Music cannot express irony, although of course the conjunction of music with words often does.

Consider the series of arias and duets in Act 2 of *La Traviata*, with all the slow pathos that Verdi can wring from a dramatic situation: never had I realized how music alone, the words aside, can change our minds about characters. Germont *père*, a self-promoting, uptight bourgeois, who worries that his son's dalliance with a courtesan will ruin the family and especially his daughter's chances for a successful marriage, sings to Violetta the most seductively melting plea: "God gave me a wonderful daughter and now you're going to ruin all of us because of your affair with my son." Of course she falls for it, gives in, renounces her love, and then dies in the last act. Whatever one thinks of Verdi's adaptation of Dumas's story, or his characterization of the fallen woman, and whatever objections one might have, as recent feminists do, to the role of woman-as-victim in much Grand Opera, music asks us to respond, even in its dramatic form when applied to human actions, to sound alone. Who would not give in to Germont's entreaty?

In the debate that goes back virtually to the beginning of opera, and carries through any collaborative effort, "classical" or popular, to match words to music, it is the music that wins the day. Consider the much-debated formula *"Prima la musica, dopo le parole"* (Music first, then the words). Often it's quoted in reverse. There's also the question of whether "prima" means first in time or first in importance. Sometimes a composer writes a score and gives it to the librettist, as Richard Rodgers did to Larry Hart. Usually it's the other way around, unless you are dealing with a rare bird like Wagner or Cole Porter, one-man shows who can think of everything simultaneously. In opera, music comes first in importance, because it carries meanings above and beyond those of the words. In this, if in nothing else, it differs from other forms of musical theater.

Like looking, listening involves focus. It can take us into a single dimension. Shut your eyes when you are left alone with noise; open your ears and the noise develops patterns. Background noise, elevator music, all the sounds we pretend to ignore but subconsciously take in, are parts of the sensuous texture of our lives. To focus on sound—especially music—can be a full-time task. How many people, especially over the age of forty, cringe at the thought of going to yet another restaurant founded on the premise that diners wish to be inundated, indeed deafened, by extraneous music? That they want a theatrical experience? Whatever happened to soft, indoor voices and civilized *sotto voce* conversation? Gone with the wind. Try to find a restaurant without music. Good luck. The pianist Alfred Brendel refuses to eat in any restaurant that plays music—especially Mozart and other classics—precisely because he finds it impossible *not* to listen to it. Deafness is not an option. The senses do not wish to multitask. At least mine do not. Some years ago I was in a small restaurant before an 8:00 p.m. curtain. We were the only guests. Music was blaring. I politely asked the waiter to turn it down or off. He returned with the maitre d', who asked what the problem was. "It's so loud, we can't hear ourselves talk," I said. "But that's the whole point," she helpfully replied. When eating these days, silence is apparently no longer golden.

Today we seldom have the choice of listening or not: we are bombarded with sounds as well as sights wherever we turn. Sitting quietly in a room, especially in a public room, is virtually impossible, unless one blocks the world out with earplugs, white noise machines, or iPods. Almost three-quarters of a century ago, the German theorist and philosopher of music Theodor Adorno wrote of background music that it "has become the music of coffee houses . . . background music means you don't have to listen. No silence surrounds and insulates it; it seeps into the hum of conversation." And he was talking about live, not canned music, about what today we could consider the innocuous strings at Florian's in Venice, or the late lamented Palm Court at the Plaza with its afternoon tea music. *Plus ça change, plus c'est la même chose!* We can only imagine what Adorno would have said about elevator music or the synthesizer, making sounds even more unreal than the pared-down arrangements of scores for cocktail orchestras. Even earlier than Adorno, George Santayana observed that people don't really even want to listen: "What most people relish is hardly music; it is rather a drowsy revery relieved by nervous thrills."

You can see tired businessmen having their drowsy reveries and doing the cultural bidding of their wives in the nation's concert halls, falling asleep in public before heading for the doors at intermission. They're just the opposite of the woman in Rodgers and Hart's "The Lady Is a Tramp": "I go to opera and stay wide awake," sang Mary Martin with a wink in her voice. She could stay awake because opera, whether for good or ill, offers food for the eyes as well as for the ears: it aspires to become entertainment rather than spiritual uplift. In *Where Angels Fear to Tread*, E. M. Forster grasped the principle and liberated his repressed, suburban English hero, Philip Herriton, through music as a social art when he attends a mediocre production of Donizetti's *Lucia di Lammermoor* in a provincial Italian hill town. The audience interrupts the soprano's famous mad scene with applause and flowers, and everyone is chatting throughout, greeting friends and neighbors, participating in the communal festivities. Opera in Italy "aims not at illusion but at entertainment," and Philip does "not want this great evening-party to turn into a prayer-meeting." He wants to take his pleasure by folding himself into the community that exists on both sides of the stage lights.

Until recently, part of opera's perennial problem was its unintelligibility: no one could understand it, often including people in whose native language it was being sung. A loud orchestra can drown out words, which disappear in space. If they're in a foreign language, they're not available to begin with. Joseph Addison remarked on the oddness of Italian opera and its great popularity in England when he wrote in *The Spectator* in 1711: "There is no question but our great grandchildren will be very curious to know the reason why their forefathers used to sit together like an audience of foreigners in their own country, and to hear whole plays acted before them in a tongue which they did not understand." If, on the other hand, opera in translation means hearing the husband in Shostakovich's *Lady Macbeth of Mtsensk* walk onstage and sing in English, "I see we're to have mushrooms for dinner tonight," then the obscurities of an unknown tongue have a great deal to recommend them. On the subject of opera in translation, one wise gentleman once said, "I don't care *what* language the opera is in as long as I *don't* understand it." This is like the bon mot of the Chicago impresario Harry Zelzer: "Good music isn't as bad as it sounds."

Unlike "the beastly Germans," Forster's Philip Herriton says that "Italians don't love music silently." Music is alive, and made more so in performance and with the help of the audience. Opera in rural Italy was a spectator sport, more like a rock concert than a church service. (If forced to choose between a rock concert and a church service, I would be hard-pressed.) Anglo-Saxon culture, in Europe as well as in the States, has always had a quasi-puritanical relationship to the dementia of opera, preferring the high-mindedness of symphonic programming. A straitlaced Yankee fear of pleasure has meant that for centuries Boston has supported a major symphony orchestra in a great hall but opera has never established a foothold there. The city still lacks a permanent company with a sizable endowment. The seats in Symphony Hall are narrow and straight-backed, only slightly more comfortable than those at Wagner's Festspielhaus in Bayreuth, which require ramrod posture and prohibit sleeping. Everyone stays wide awake there. They are worshipping at the shrine of art on the *heilige Hügel.*

And probably not since the nineteenth century, when Paganini, Chopin, and Liszt famously made ladies swoon in overheated drawing rooms and salons, have there been instrumental musicians who have commanded the star power of Caruso and Pavarotti, Callas and Sutherland, Geraldine Farrar, who inspired worshipful Gerryflappers, or Dame Nellie Melba, for whom both the toast and the peach dish were named. As early as 1850, when P. T. Barnum brought Jenny Lind on her first American tour, he kept close watch on the box office and the marketing opportunities: "Milliners, mantua-makers, and shop-keeepers vied with each other in calling her attention to their wares, delighted if, in return, they could receive her autograph acknowledgment." No pianist today can quite match the Swedish nightingale as a source of celebrity endorsements.

The flip side of staying awake—at opera or in the concert hall—is dozing, and many people do it not only because they are tired but because (let us now confess it), music is sometimes boring. I am not the first to make this observation. In an 1888 essay, "Boredom in Music," Camille Bellaigue says that he intends to talk not about the boredom music can express but that which it inspires, in the same way we discuss religion and nature and love in music. Bellaigue makes two important points. The first is that music, especially bad music, like all mediocre art and artists, is not indispensable. A mediocre doctor or lawyer still has a necessary place in society. But a mediocre pianist? And the second—a version of an earlier point of mine—has to do with noise. Music is sound, and sound is noise, and "disagreeable noise is an odious thing. At least the other arts are silent. Besides, you can put down a volume of poetry or turn your eyes away from a statue or a picture, but you can't escape music."

Forster, again, gets it right when he observes (in "Not Listening to Music") that most of the time when supposed to be listening he's really woolgathering, distracted by people's appearance, or thinking of something else. Who has not had the same feeling: "A classical audience is surely the plainest collection of people anywhere assembled for any common purpose; contributing my quota, I have the right to point this out." And when thinking about the mind's inevitable wandering, he distinguishes between ideal listening, to the music itself, and hearing "music that reminds me of something." Only the first is of genuine value. He thinks of Monet when listening to Debussy (as he thought of Debussy when looking at Monet). In other words, in 1939, Forster turns his back on his earlier character Helen Schlegel, in the 1910 novel *Howards End*, and sides squarely with her sister Margaret, who's all in favor of purity in the arts, of each one keeping to its own place: "What is the good of the ear if it tells you the same as the eye? . . . If Monet's really Debussy, and Debussy's really Monet, neither gentleman is worth his salt." Anglo-Saxon common sense wins the day. So much for what we call synaesthesia, even though some psychologists have suggested that some people's brains in fact work this way. P. E. Vernon, a research fellow at Cambridge in both psychology and sacred music, found that 6 percent of his subjects associated sounds with colors. One man hears A major and sees green, then remembers that green is A major, so develops a kind of absolute pitch through the agency of color.

Luckily, most of us aren't like that fellow. You can escape music, of course, by falling asleep or turning off the radio or inserting earplugs. But when listened to carefully, music does all the things the musicians, composers, theorists, and ordinary partisans have been saying for millennia. Here's where reproduced rather than live music has the decided advantage, although it doesn't deliver the thrill of a great live performance. Everyone is aware of a neighbor—or a whole house—coughing and sneezing, or snoring; of a woman who rattles her jewels or unwraps a piece of candy; of a floor creaking as someone makes a belated entrance; of people behind you chatting volubly and offering their opinions as if they were sitting in their living room; of a subway train below or an airplane overhead adding its own sonic two cents to the sound. And of the cell phone that rings inopportunely.

Listening with your Platonic ear, which cuts out extraneous sounds and allows you to hear only what the composer asks for, forces you to enter the wordless world of harmony and pitch, of orchestration, dynamics, rhythm, and melody, or what is left of it. (Unless the composer is John Cage, who has choreographed silence in order to alert us to the necessity of the extraneous.) We try hard to ignore distractions and focus on music. "To attend," after all, does not mean only to get dressed up (nowadays we don't even have to do that), go somewhere, buy a ticket, and sit down at a performance. More important, it means quite simply to pay attention.

For those who listen well, in real isolation or joined in isolation with others in a hall, music without words has as its primary purpose the transmission of what the philosopher Susanne K. Langer termed "presentational symbolism," which she distinguished from "discursive symbolism." Through its own forms, music articulates the forms of feeling, not necessarily the feelings of composer, performer, or even audience members, but feeling almost as an abstraction. Music, she says, does not cause or cure feelings but expresses them logically through its own wordless structures. Music articulates what language cannot set forth. Agreeing with Wagner, Langer says that music conveys what cannot be spoken, primarily the shape or "the morphology of feeling." Although the essential musical relationships—tension and resolution—lack any assigned connotation or meaning, our sentient experience while listening resembles the rise and fall, the rhythm and interruptions, of feelings in our mental life. A change in key may convey a new idea, although its effect strikes us below the level of consciousness, and in Langer's words, "outside the pale of discursive thinking," where it "produces some peculiar effects we mistake" for feelings because it resembles feelings and provokes them.

In "Peter Quince at the Clavier," Wallace Stevens says, "Music is feeling, then, not sound," but this is not entirely right. Music is the sound that conveys something *like* feeling and then replicates it within its listeners. This is one reason that the best music criticism, even more than the criticism of literature and painting, relies necessarily on metaphor, imagery, and impression. An analysis of structure—first theme, variations, second theme, resolution, harmonic dissonances, augmented sixths and diminished sevenths—in the technical vocabulary of the musical theorist can tell us what is happening but not why or to what effect. Even musicians themselves must resort to our common language. Here, for instance, is Gounod discussing Palestrina in his 1896 *Memoirs*: "This music—severe, ascetic, horizontal, and calm, like the boundary of the ocean; monotonous by dint of serenity; antisensual and yet so intense in its contemplativeness that it sometimes attains to the ecstatic—made at first a strange, almost disagreeable impression." Snatching a metaphor from the realm of the visible,

Gounod finds language to describe the peculiar auditory effect of his predecessor's harmonies.

Forster, thinking again of "that imp of the concert hall, inattention," says he is easily sidetracked from "music itself" to "music that reminds me of something," especially when he reads program notes or programmatic musical explanations. Beethoven's "Coriolan" overture was forever ruined for him because Wagner had written about it programmatically. Forster: "I have lost my Coriolanus. Its largeness and freedom have gone. The exquisite sounds have been hardened like a road that has been tarred for traffic." There's the writer with his metaphor again; will it be possible to hear Beethoven's overture without thinking of a paved road overrun by trucks?

Forster avoided such extraneous woolgathering by playing the piano himself, something he persisted in doing even though he played more poorly from year to year. Precisely because he had to focus on eyes and fingers, on reading the score and making music, Forster attended. He concludes, "Even when people play as badly as I do, they should continue: it will help them to listen." Like me, he became a better part of the audience. A mediocre pianist, *pace* Bellaigue, does have a place in society. It's the same in any art: the Sunday painter can emulate but never duplicate her favorite; a dancer can take lots of lessons and still not become Fred Astaire, but he comes to appreciate Astaire all the more for that very reason.

Listen: a writer can doodle, free-associate, find words, and put them together in the attempt to "find his own voice," as they tell novices to do in "creative writing" courses. Few people ever make the discovery, of course; their fingerprints and DNA may be unique, but most people seldom reach that point at which they find in words their own best, unique selves. The metaphor in this hoary cliché from writing courses contains, however, an essential truth about the relationship between writing and speech, between reading and hearing. A writer is a talker whose work must embody at some level the image of a person speaking. Writers talk silently. Readers listen as their eyes scan the page. Most writers continue to try to find their audience but also, more important, their voices, or their selves, as if on a quest for something long lost.

From listening we move to making music, and from attempting to make music we can move on to listening better, more sympathetically and critically. From reading as a precursor, we move on to writing (see chapter 7) and whether or not that writing ever interests anyone else, we can return to reading with greater appreciation.

6 Swimming

The most famous swimmer among the English poets, George Gordon, Lord Byron, wrote a single jaunty poem on the activity—actually, one of the many activities—that made him legendary throughout Europe in his lifetime. "After Swimming from Sestos to Abydos" revises and updates the old myth of Leander, who braved the Hellespont every evening to visit Hero on the other side. Whereas the lissome Greek swam for love, Byron allows that he, "degenerate modern youth," aimed for fame and glory on the one-mile swim he took on May 3, 1810, in typically strong currents. And where Leander perished in his pursuit—which Christopher Marlowe treats with fervor and high camp in his luscious mini-epic Elizabethan poem "Hero and Leander"—Byron comes out of his adventure with nothing nobler than "the ague," a cold.

The man who swam up the Grand Canal in Venice in three and three-quarter hours after a night of revelry on the Lido took to the water for the same reason that he took so easily to horseback: he could do anything but walk normally. Swimming hid a congenital deformity and allowed him to forget it temporarily. Cursed with a club-foot, for which he always blamed his mother, Byron became both the beau ideal of the Romantic lover and a classic case of an overcompensator. Buoyancy of all kinds—sangfroid and physical bravery, flamboyant wit and aristocratic ease—was in his case the other side of angst, gloom, and sinking torpor. I wonder whether swimmers, regardless of the isolation they endure in the pursuit of their pleasure, aren't by nature more cheerful than other people. After all, what does "buoyant" mean?

With Byron swimming really enters English literature. The nineteenth century is full of swimming writers, most notably Clough and Swinburne, the latter of whom preferred dangerous coasts, but there's not much of it before Byron aside from Marlowe's description of Leander, deliciously tickled and fondled by Neptune, who swims underneath him in the sea:

> He clapt his plumpe cheekes, with his tresses playd,
> And smiling wantonly, his love bewrayed.
> He watcht his armes, and as they opend wide,
> At every stroke, betwixt them he would slide,
> And steale a kisse, and then run out and daunce,
> And as he turnd, cast many a lustful glaunce,
> And threw him gawdie toies to please his eie,
> And dive into the water, and there prie
> Upon his brest, his thighs, and every lim,
> And up againe, and close beside him swim.
>
> ll. 665–74

By and large, even after the nineteenth century, writers have tended to ignore the activity: not just poets, but even fiction writers and journalists. For every sportswriter with an interest in baseball, boxing, or football (Roger Angell, Joyce Carol Oates, and George Plimpton) there has been almost no one to testify to the beauties and pleasures of this loneliest of physical activities, as either an observer or a participant.

Almost no one: one recent anthology, *Splash: Great Writing about Swimming* (1996), edited by Laurel Blossom with an introduction by the late Plimpton, who never met a sport he didn't like, contains some wonderful modern selections, including John Cheever's "The Swimmer," that eerily chilling allegory of a man who swims across the suburban pools of his neighborhood only to discover that he has grown old and forlorn in his quest to get home. This is the most famous contemporary American swimming piece. Blossom's anthology has other, unexpected delights, poems by Philip Booth, James Dickey, A. E. Housman, Mary Oliver, Anne Sexton, and Stevie Smith, and prose from Jack London and Doris Lessing. Perhaps most touching is Laurie Colwin's "Wet," about a man who learns that his wife sneaks off every day for a secret, private hour that excludes him. The story ends: "What had grieved him was simply a fact: every day of her life she would be at some point damp, then drying, and for one solid time, wet." The revelation shocks, even terrifies.

The reasons for swimming's relative neglect in writing are not hard to find. By definition, swimming excludes husbands, lovers, everyone else in the world, indeed everything else except one's thoughts. Like Cheever's hero, Colwin's main character, the non-swimmer, has an existential crisis (what is it about swimming that provokes these?) when he realizes the essential isolation of his wife underwater. For her part, the wife has no problems at all with it, because swimming keeps her sane.

The activity suffers from other kinds of inattention as well. Swimming, everyone seems to agree, makes for a bad spectator sport, Michael Phelps notwithstanding. It is boring for the prospective audience as well as for the participants. Where there is pleasure to be gained from watching a runner in full stride, especially in a sprint, but even in the marathon, you can't really see swimming. The body is submerged and only partially visible. And even when visible, the activity is not necessarily always lovely. Like some runners, some swimmers have ungainly styles, like the windmill arms of Olympian Janet Evans. But speed, not beauty or technique, wins the race, and different folks have different strokes. Television underwater cameras have changed our perspective, but nevertheless the event remains largely unwatched.

Unwatchable? Not entirely. At least one notable contemporary poem has been written about swimming. Charles Tomlinson, an Englishman who by his own admission can't swim at all, wrote "Swimming Chenango Lake" during a stint teaching at Colgate University in upstate New York in the late 1960s. It is a poem at once spectatorial and physical, that is, it gives a sense of what it's like to be in a New England lake in the fall as well as to observe a lone swimmer take a last plunge before winter bars him from more of the same. Having read "the water's autumnal hesitations / A wealth of ways," the swimmer enters into and contributes to the water's geometry as he "scissors the waterscape apart / And sways it to tatters":

> *For to swim is also to take hold*
> *On water's meaning, to move in its embrace*
> *And to be, between grasp and grasping, free.*

The swimmer becomes part of the element that supports him, part of an ever-changing geometry through which he slices and which then corrects itself as he moves past. The human body is 70 percent water: swimming returns us to ourselves. The swimmer's action combines fact ("grasp") and process ("grasping"); it requires submission that then becomes liberation. You move beyond yourself and leave no trace. Swimming frees you from the world.

I think of Tomlinson's poem every time I swim outdoors, the sun on my back, shedding its rays on the water around, before, and beneath me. In middle age I began to suffer from a modest case of heliophobia (a word of my own invention), brought on by pesky, small pre-cancerous growths on my temples and forehead, which has prevented me from venturing out too often unless the skies are almost totally overcast. But earlier, in 1976, while I was still fearless, I had an experience that has stayed with me. I was swimming not in a lake but in a public pool near the Charles River in downtown Boston. Labor Day had passed; the pool was ending its season. Children had returned to school, and I was the only person in the water on a crisp, early September afternoon. The pool was sorry, old and ill maintained, with crumbling tile, the kind you find in every major city, a sad remnant of some well-intentioned municipal public-works project. It was shallow, but it was fifty meters long, the perfect length for the serious lap swimmer because it allows you to build momentum and pace, and to turn less rather than more frequently. It makes you get—as they didn't say then—into the zone, and getting into the zone is what swimming, like long-distance running, is all about. The day was cool; the equinox was approaching; the sun had begun its descent. In the water I had the exquisite sensation that the entire world belonged to me, that like Robert Frost's unnamed character in "The Most of It," I "kept the universe alone." There was nothing but me and the cosmos, together.

Swimming, unique among physical activities, diminishes if not entirely eliminates the sense of sight, our primary means of engagement with the physical world. You see the sides of the pool, the bottom, the lane markers; you get momentary glimpses of the world as you breathe or raise your head above the water as you turn, but by and large vision is kept at a minimum. Mostly you witness the shimmer of light all around you. Hearing, too, undergoes a change. Unless you're the kind of desperate person who wears a Swim-Man, the underwater equivalent of a Walkman headset, all you hear are the constant rush of the water, and your own movement and breathing as you glide through. Of the senses, it is touch most of all that defines the swimmer's activity, and even "touch" is virtually metaphorical, because nothing solid exists as you pull, push, and otherwise make your way through a fluid medium. When you are swimming outside, of course, weather plays a delicious part in the body's responsiveness. You can swim in the rain, feeling one kind of water hit you from above while moving through another kind of water. You can see—or catch short glimpses of—clouds passing across the sun. In streams, ponds, or the ocean you can proceed suddenly from one temperature to another, as currents cut in. Like all physical activities, swimming asks of us that we attend not only to our bodies but also to their relation to the physical world beyond us. For Paul Valéry, the analogy was to sex: "To plunge into water, to move one's whole body, from head to toe, in its wild and graceful beauty; to twist about in its pure depths, this is for me a delight only comparable to love." Water buoys and supports; it also resists. To swim, as Tomlinson says, is to take hold of water's meaning, and in that meaning we come to learn something about ourselves, our world, and the relations between the two.

Swimming does not come naturally to anyone, except perhaps to those newborns whose mothers decide to return them to a new equivalent of amniotic fluid as soon as they emerge from the womb. Otherwise, it's an activity fraught with fear—of sinking, drowning, losing sight, losing control—until one learns to give oneself in or up to water's buoyancy. Until the mid-fifties, when the Salk vaccine more or less eliminated the polio virus, public swimming pools, like drinking fountains, were places burdened with danger. Unlike walking, which no one requires teaching to learn how to do, or even running, which all kids do automatically, swimming requires not only submission and instruction but also a kind of courage. Some people can remember their first baptismal dips or educative experiences. I cannot. I suppose they took place at summer day camp under the supervision of a patient counselor, or perhaps even at the hands of my own unathletic parents at a local pool or at the beach in Atlantic City. I know I made it from one end of the pool to the other in high school gym class. We had to pass a test. For the only time in my life I executed a perfect dive, and swam a flawless lap. Getting a grade was my sole incentive. I know I splashed in backyard and country-club pools when I was a teenager, but I also know that I was by no stretch of the imagination a swimmer.

To this bookish youth, a transformative revelation occurred when, at the age of twenty-three, I decided that I had a body that required tending to. Does one *have* a body? Does one inhabit the body, a soul within a carapace? Are you your body? I came to ponder, underwater, the interesting philosophical dimensions of the question. In graduate school I was living literally next door to the university swimming pool. Swimming seemed the easiest and the most expedient exercise, one that depended, unlike competitive games, on no one else's schedule. For sheer convenience, running or walking is always the easiest thing to do: neither weather nor location should ever inhibit you. Swimming demands a place and also necessary scheduling, but since I was free at ten in the morning when the pool opened, and since it was never crowded at that hour, I had no excuse other than laziness for not doing it.

In those days, swimming, like exercise in general, had not reached as far into the national consciousness as it has since. Everyone knew that exercising was healthy, but no one discussed it. No one was obsessed, and no one talked about endorphins. If you wanted to do something, you did it. Running shoes had not become a highly specialized, scientifically controlled, and commercially advertised product. Ergonomics was not yet a word in the layman's vocabulary. Varsity swimmers must have worn racing suits, by Speedo or some comparable company, but ordinary people wore what were called plain old-fashioned swimming trunks. Or, as in my case, they wore nothing at all. The university pool was all-male. It was Harvard's equivalent of Oxford's Parson's Pleasure, and in the days before the contemporary modesty that obtains in many male locker rooms, men went unashamedly naked. Women had a separate, far from equal, facility elsewhere. The drill was simple and ancient, like the building where we swam. You undressed in the dingy locker room with rusty lockers, you showered, you walked through a largely symbolic footbath, and there you were: six lanes, twenty-five yards long, in front of you. There may have been lane dividers—I cannot recall—but you simply found yourself a place and you dove or, like me, slid into the water and pushed off. On my first day I made it to the other end and stopped, feeling dizzy. I paused, regained my energy, and swam back. Not knowing how to breathe properly, I didn't put my head in the water, but managed something between an inept crawl and an inefficient doggy paddle. One full lap—two lengths—fifty yards. I exited, feeling a bit nauseated (had I eaten breakfast too soon before exercising?), and made it to the toilet just in time to vomit.

That was Day One. Day Two: I returned and managed two laps, with no adverse physical effects other than slight muscle pains and a bit less dizziness. I was on my way. I hardly thought about what I was doing. In fact, I barely knew what I was doing. I could improvise a path from one end of the pool to the other, but I still didn't breathe properly for some months; I must have had a fear of keeping my ungoggled eyes in the chlorinated water. At some point I bought goggles and taught myself how to turn my head from one side to the other, but I would have looked pretty foolish and ungraceful to anyone who happened to watch me flail my way back and forth, up and down. Still, one perseveres. After several weeks I found myself—unnauseated and undizzy—gaining strength and endurance. I managed to set goals for myself, modest ones of course, and to meet them. Was I becoming a jock? I, whose idea of pleasure in school and college was sitting quietly in a room reading and smoking? I always relished the famous bon mot of Robert Maynard Hutchins, president of the University of Chicago, that whenever he felt the urge to exercise he lay down and waited for it to pass. Never run when you can walk; never walk when you can be driven. A college teacher of mine, a nice Jewish fellow from the Bronx, told a similar story. When he was an undergraduate in the early 1950s, he belonged to an organization called Exercisers Anonymous: whenever you felt the urge to sweat you dialed a number, and within minutes some helpful agents would arrive at your doorstep, bearing a bottle of whiskey, some cigarettes, and a deck of cards.

I was hardly a jock. But, like any solo exercise, swimming, at least as I practiced it, is noncompetitive, so I didn't feel threatened by anyone else. I also took equal, virtually inexplicable pleasure in the simple idea that I was doing it. (I had the same pleasure when I learned ancient Greek.) I had no delusion or even a thought that medals lay in my future. I amazed myself, no one else. One day I noticed that I was swimming between Erik Erikson, on one side of me, and John Kenneth Galbraith on the other. The former performed an elegant breaststroke, never putting his leonine head of snow-white locks into the water; the latter, what seemed like all eight feet of him, simply pushed off from one end and arrived at the other immediately, effortlessly. There we were: world-famous psychologist and biographer, world-famous economist and ambassador, and I, world-ignored nobody. The Harvard swimming pool was more like an extension of the Faculty Club than it was a venue for serious athletic prowess. Even when women were admitted, the genial informality remained. All this was to change some years later when Harvard built the Blodgett Pool, a state-of-the-art facility that allowed casual swimmers to share space with competitors, divers in their separate well, and physical education classes. In retrospect I am glad for the absence of really good swimmers who might have embarrassed me. I would have been scared off, as I had been as a child by those ferocious public school gym teachers, all of whom either were or might have been ex-military men who took less interest in the pleasures of bodily exercise than in the sadistic kicks they got from putting us through our daily paces. Coming to the pool as an adult, and of my own free will, made all the difference in my sense of my body and my relation to it, or of its relation to the rest of me.

Swimming is an act of imaginative adventure: "The experience of swimming is both sexual and spiritual. The sensation of water flowing over the body is dynamic, erotic, enlivening, and yet it awakens, at every moment, our consciousness of the fragility of our breath." So said Australian swimmer and early film star Annette Kellerman. Water supports and resists, and there's no one lonelier, even a runner of the longest distances, than a swimmer. Sensory diminishment, or the transformation of the senses underwater, forces you in upon what inner resources you have. The imagination complements the body as you work through the water. John Nabor, a 1976 Olympic medalist, has remarked upon the relative gregariousness of competitive divers, who preen, strut, and sit around between dives in hot tubs and Jacuzzis to keep their muscles loose. Swimmers, on the other hand, are by definition loners: "Swimmers don't have anyone to commune with except themselves . . . Nothing but the rush of water in their ears, hour after hour in practice. Many of them sing to themselves, to pass the time." I must have been on to something—not knowing at the time that I had placed myself in the company of my betters—because I too was singing.

Swimming gave me, and continues to give, the chance to sing to myself, to recite poems, to plan my future, and to review the past. To enter a meditative Zen-like state as I count my strokes per lap, like the Buddhist practice known as *kinhin*, matching your steps to your breath as you walk around a room. And in another way, as well, I was part of this company of self-reliant loners: apparently, the best swimmers rarely excel at other sports, because their bodies are too oddly developed, with long, pliable muscles and large hands and feet, the prime requirements for competitors. They don't adapt well to land games. Not that I ever thought of grooming myself for other activities, and not that my hands and feet are long, or my muscles especially pliable.

What is true for ordinary swimmers like me, especially people who confine themselves to laps in a pool, is not necessarily so for open-sea, deepwater swimmers. I doubt that Matthew Webb, the first man to swim the English Channel—from Dover to Cap Gris—on August 24, 1875, was singing to himself during his twenty-two hours in the water, and certainly not in 1883, when he died in the rapids above Niagara Falls. Like all long-distance swimmers, Gertrude Ederle, the first woman to do the Channel, in 1926, had to pay more attention to tides, temperatures, and floating debris than to the workings of her psyche.

According to Mark Spitz, swimming is perfect for narcissists. Like the mind, the body is self-absorbed. Spitz calls swimming the only sport that puts a competitor on a pedestal—the racing block—even before he begins, where he "is introduced and applauded. He hasn't even done anything. Instant recognition. That's so much of what an athlete wants. Then he gets rewarded immediately afterwards. It would be terrible if he got the award the next day. He might forget what he got it for." Spitz makes it seem as if long underwater sessions have affected the poor athlete's mind, as if short-term memory has begun to vanish.

Even more than to narcissists, swimming appeals to obsessives and dreamers. Charles Sprawson, whose *Haunts of the Black Masseur* (1993) remains the single best book devoted to the activity, observes that both opium addicts and swimmers "tended to be solitary, remote figures, who felt themselves superior to dull, conventional minds." Both sorts of person were absorbed by the strangeness of their experience, and it is no wonder that swimming gained new currency among the eccentric English in the nineteenth century. What is oddest about swimming is that it has, in fact, a history—a story that has changed over time and in different places. In ancient Greece, it was a skill that fathers were expected to teach their children. Most pictorial representations show swimmers doing a sidestroke, or in the middle of a swan dive. The dive suggests that there may have been informal competitions, but we have no records or information about spectators. Different strokes, like poetic stanzas, move in and out of favor. The swimming competition at the first modern Olympics (Athens, 1896) was held in the Bay of Zéa at Piraeus. Distances were marked by the spacing of the barges that also held spectators and judges. There was no division among strokes: the first event was a 100-meter race, and the breaststroke was by far the favored technique. (The backstroke was introduced in 1900, the Australian crawl a bit later.) The only American entrant was not used to cold water, having spent his time in pools; he dove in, screamed, and went back to the float he'd just jumped from. Most of the men were naked, except one Hungarian and the delicate American.

Apparently some version of the breaststroke held sway longest in the West. One theory is that it evolved after the fall of Rome, when water either became dirtier or was considered a source of plague and disease. Hand motions held the body above water, and kept water from entering the mouth. I suspect that the metaphorical phrase "keeping your head above water" must have originated for this practical reason, although by now we mostly keep our heads fully submerged when we swim, except when on our backs. Elizabethans preferred a doggy paddle, replaced by the frog or breaststroke, what Webb used. In 1726 the young Ben Franklin swam in the Thames from Chelsea down to Blackfriars just for the fun of it, although we're not sure how he did it. What we know as the crawl, or freestyle, emerged at the end of the nineteenth century. American Indians, in competition with English swimmers in London in 1845, used an overarm, flailing windmill stroke, which inspired Johnny Weissmuller much later. The Hawaiian Duke Kahanamoku streamlined the crawl. By the time Ederle swam the Channel, she beat the men's record by two hours, swimming the crawl the whole way.

Melchisedek Thevenot wrote one of the first manuals, *Art of Swimming*, in 1696. Published first in French, then in English three years later, it reminds us of swimming's past and of how that past differs from its present. People swam less for pleasure, pure and simple, than for cleanliness, commerce (diving for pearls, for example), self-preservation in battle, or when they happened to find themselves, unfortunately, on a sinking ship. The instructions and the pictures are actually hilarious by our standards. The actual teaching deals almost exclusively with the breaststroke as the default mode. The book also features a mini-treatise on a kind of armless elementary backstroke, with a frog kick, performed with your hands on your stomach. Chapter XV, "To Swim on the Belly, Holding Both Your Hands Still," teaches how to swim on your belly with your hands behind your head or on your back. The action is all in the legs. It's really just glorified floating. The author observes: "This way of swimming may be useful, in case of accident, as the cramp, etc., should happen to your arms, or if you were forced on occasion to swim with your hands tied behind you, or in case you were a prisoner, and your life depended on it." Ah yes: a useful skill. The following chapter gives direction on how "to Carry the Left Leg in the Right Hand," helpful—again—in case of cramp or gout, "or if one leg should be entangled among the weeds." My favorite? Chapter XXVII, which, having reminded us that an expert can stand, sit, lie, or move through water, shows us how "To Cut the Nails of the Toes in the Water."

Although we know that the ancient Greeks enjoyed swimming, the activity experienced changes in popularity. Under Christianity it declined, to be revived with spectacular energy at the start of the nineteenth century. In Britain, the homoerotic, or at least the homosocial, angle was strong, as it was in Germany. Cyril Connolly summed up the old Etonian tradition in a prewar journal: "A fusion of my old trinity, grace, greenness, and security" came from his sense of the tradition of "two friends going down to bathe." Hellenic worship of the body and pastoral sinlessness merged, at least in the imagination. Bloomsbury swam. Rose Macaulay as well as Virginia Woolf swam naked with Rupert Brooke before the Great War. Iris Murdoch was one of the last great English river swimmers.

For all these people—as for us who have swum after them on our backs or stomachs—water has cleansing, purifying powers. *"Ariston men hudor"* ("Water is best," especially when cold): the swimming society of old Etonians took as their motto the opening line of Pindar's first Olympian Ode. The swimming rite, compounded equally of physical and spiritual parts, continues to provide a sense of awakening even for those of us who resort to the enclosed spaces of indoor pools rather than the *loci amoeni* (the "pleasant places" in Latin pastoral poetry) of springs, lakes, and oceans, all with their attendant deities. But in addition to its physical and quasi-religious aspects, swimming allows something else: the expansion of the mind in the act of contemplation. This it shares, of course, with long-distance running, and especially the meditative impulse of the mind thinking in the act of walking. But because of the sensory transformation inherent in water, the mind works even more abstractly when the body is submerged.

Ludwig Wittgenstein articulated the connection best: "Just as one's body has a natural tendency towards the surface and one has to make an exertion to get to the bottom—so it is with thinking." One might also argue the opposite: the body unaccustomed to the water has a tendency to sink; only buoyancy, innate or learned, can keep it up. And with thought, the same is true: we divide our focus between what remains on the surface and what seems to lie below it, seldom realizing that the very metaphor we use to describe the mind's realm has an analogy in water and our experience of it.

Oliver Sacks, the distinguished polymath neurologist with expertise ranging across many scientific and humanistic disciplines, has described in a sweet autobiographical essay, "Water Babies," the joy that comes from playing in and with the buoyant medium that supports the swimmer. More important, he describes how the mind-altering properties of swimming can get thinking going as nothing else can. "Ecstasy," he calls it—that word whose origin in Greek refers to standing outside of oneself: "There was a total engagement in the act of swimming, in each stroke, and at the same time the mind could float free, become spellbound, in a state like a trance." In such trances one dreams, one composes—poems, songs, lectures, it hardly matters what—one even sings to oneself. Large swatches of the Gilbert and Sullivan operettas I memorized for no reason in adolescence have passed through my mind's mouth during a ninety-minute swim. Who knows where he might discover utility? Sacks, also, aligns swimming with "*musical* activities": flowing, buoying, suspending in its dynamics. Swimmers pay attention to rhythm, much as dancers do. Like Sacks, an athlete engaged in any endorphin-producing activity knows the fretful nervousness that ensues when he is deprived of the source of his euphoria. "Healthy addiction" sounds like a paradox, but to be addicted to the natural physical high that comes from exercise has got to be one of the best, and certainly the cheapest, thrills available to us. The life of the senses leads to kinds of pleasure that reach far beyond them.

Nothing lasts forever. Even those daily routines that give pleasure bend to the fact of change. At some point one feels a desire to improve or to vary the pace. When you walk, you do so out of a combination of pedestrian necessity and a search for pleasure. It seldom matters—unless you are race-walking or pumping up the cardiovascular juices—whether you improve. But like a pianist who starts with Czerny's finger exercises and moves to simple Mozart sonatas, complex Bach fugues, and large-handed Liszt or Scriabin chords, an athlete wants to expand technique, to improve performance. Swimming is far from natural, and one can always get better. Not that I have ever felt the competitive urge that would drive me to master classes, age-group competitions, or to entertain middle-aged, Walter Mitty–like fantasies of winning a trophy. The desire is, pure and simple, to advance. Not merely to go faster, but to increase the thrill that comes from more grace and a deeper engagement with the water itself. To become a more aquatic mammal.

So, thirty-eight years after entering the Harvard pool by myself, and more than a half century after first encountering the water in some far-off, unremembered place and time, I began to take lessons. Having been buoyant all those years, I wanted to find additional support for my natural inclination. Greater speed, greater effectiveness, more buoyancy: more pleasure, greater happiness. Or so I thought. I engaged the services of a former varsity swimmer who gives private and group instruction. Anyone who has gone from working out solo in a gym to using a personal trainer will know exactly what happened. From thinking of myself for so long as competent I now had to undo decades of bad habits, and to relearn almost from square one the sport, the art I once claimed to have mastered.

Everything seemed to be wrong with me and my movement: the angle at which my arms entered the water; the placement of my head when I turned to breathe; the position of my body in the water; the way I pushed off from the wall; the pull of my hands to initiate and finish a stroke; my kick. What did I have going for me? Well, at least I have endurance, I thought, having spent countless sessions swimming nonstop for more than an hour. In fact, after being put through one kind of drill or another ("Go out at 100 percent; come back at 80 percent; rest ten seconds, and then repeat"), I could barely catch my breath. Speed training, the aquatic equivalent of a runner's wind sprints; new drills and exercises; attachments such as paddles, straps, flippers, kickboards, and pull-buoys: all these new games and new toys helped to improve everything I was doing.

But the work was neither a pleasure, except after I had finished, nor an easy task to accomplish. For one thing, the sheer force of habit and muscle memory ensures that unless you focus very hard on an instruction ("Chin down" or "Chest out" or "Make sure your right arm doesn't slice across your body"), you tend to revert to the default mode, to the bad old ways. The skill demands concentration. But how many things can you think of simultaneously? In my case, it was only one. So I had to make the not uncommon request of my coach that she give me just a single item to think about for a certain number of yards. "Focus on your right hand," "Breathe on every third stroke," "Keep your heels above the water line," and so on. The fun was evaporating, quickly.

And another thing: this equivalent of going back to elementary school puts a teacher like me into the instructive position of becoming a student again. When what he is studying is something for which he lacks a natural gift, when he must learn to do something with and for and to his body rather than his mind, the experience is, to put it mildly, humbling. I felt, as I did on the dance floor, like a slow, untalented learner whose teachers had to demonstrate extra kindness and sympathy. I have learned more about teaching from those coaches I have had (dancing and yoga instructors, a personal trainer, and now a swimming tutor) than from any of my academic colleagues, for the simple reasons that I must pay more attention to my lowly student status and they must find the appropriate metaphors—in addition to technical and scientific terms—to describe exactly what they want me to do. In order to improve my technique, I had to learn how to listen to instructions and internalize them. I had to follow orders. I had to give up improvisation. I had to become serious.

By making me concentrate, this whole adventure also had the unwonted but not undesirable effect of making me *think* about my body and its activity. This is precisely the kind of thinking I had successfully avoided for decades. It's what I went to swimming to escape *from*. When swimming before, I had allowed myself the luxury of daydreaming, of finding the meditative zone that best suited my sanguine, lackadaisical temperament. If a thing is worth doing, I have always thought, it's worth doing badly. Why put yourself through pain? Why cause stress? Why *work*? Decades ago I had reached the point of being able to slide into a pool, swim at a constant pace for long periods of time without stopping, and climb out refreshed and relaxed. Under the new regime everything changed. At the end of thirty minutes I was panting; the following day previously unknown or dormant muscles ached and burned. My body felt leaden, stony, dead. I was making progress.

For me, the very fun of swimming had been equivalent to that of walking: it fostered and deepened the life of the mind. It cultivated the imagination. Now I had to readjust my thinking about thinking. Intensity replaced mechanical relaxation. No more Gilbert and Sullivan, no more recitation of poems, no more making class plans for my students or lists of things to do. No more naming all the American presidents and their running mates in order, along with their opponents. I had to focus entirely on my right shoulder, my thighs, my left pinkie, the angle of my chin, or whichever body part was the object of intense temporary scrutiny. I had to concentrate on torso rotation, on my core muscles, on my glide, on the catch-and-pull of my stroke. The body has a mind of its own, and that mind had to be studied and put through its paces. Life in the pool used to give me an enchanted, hypnotic, and transcendent escape; on a long swim, I could feel my pulse speed up gradually and my blood pressure decline. Practice made better, if not perfect, but it also stole away swimming's intrinsic mystery. Now all was changed: every inch of my body worked at closer to peak levels, and my mind had ceased to function except in relation to the job at hand.

Swimming had become, in fact, labor. Previously, I left work behind me when I entered the pool, other than as something to think about with equanimity. Now I had a new kind of toil, whose results came often in inverse proportion to the immediate gratification I received. Swimming became a science; I had to learn hydrodynamics, streamlining, propulsion, laws of energy and physics, none of which held any immediate appeal for me. And I had to swim in consultation with someone else. Whereas before I could welcome, and take refuge in, the sheer silence of staying underwater, now I had conversations with my smiling, coffee-sipping coach after every 50 or 100 or 200 yards. I had to attend to her words even when I was breathlessly panting. Being in the water came to resemble being out of it. Years ago I was talking to a student of mine, an Adonis of an Olympic swimmer who had just finished his collegiate swimming career. I asked whether his last meet was a bittersweet event, whether he felt an anticlimax. He agreed that it was, and he did. "You'll keep swimming for fun from here on?" I inquired. "Are you out of your mind?" he said, "I've been doing this since I was five years old and I hope never to have to get into the water again."

Eventually I achieved a synthesis. From the unmitigated pleasure of an hour's swim, the equivalent of a leisurely, old-fashioned stroll in the park during which the mind can wander freely with the body, I moved to the torture of drills, the counterpart of those flash cards you use when studying a new language or the constant exercises of verbs and tenses and moods that you finally internalize through practice. Then, after great pain, you reach the higher plateau. Without having to think, you automatically find the right idioms and tenses. You emerge proficient.

The life of the body turns out to resemble, rather than differ from, the life of the mind. What I learned in my coaching sessions gradually interwove itself into my stroke, into my entire performance. Concentration vanished, or at least found a different object. I internalized my lessons and no longer had to think about discrete body parts. I became more intimate with the water and with myself. Instruction had liberated me, and I returned to the water confident that I could resume—on those days when I didn't want to think too hard about my stroke but, instead, merely count the numbers—my internal singing of G&S patter songs, my recitation of poems, my gradual raising myself into a higher spiritual realm. I became more buoyant, in spirit as well as in body. Swimming keeps me happy.

7) *Writing*

I'll start with two of the famous bons mots: "Writing is easy: All you do is sit staring at a blank sheet of paper until drops of blood form on your forehead" (attributed to Gene Fowler and Red Barber); "No man but a blockhead ever wrote, except for money" (Samuel Johnson). More than any other activity I write about in this book—reading, walking, looking, dancing, listening, and swimming—writing causes pain and frustration well before it gives satisfaction. And although composers, choreographers, and painters probably endure comparable fallow periods, no one seems to suffer from creative blockage more than writers. At least they devote a lot of time and energy to talking about their inability to write. Why does anyone do it when the rewards appear incommensurate with the effort? Writer's blocks and blockheads: they make an impressive pair. Writing about writing, I now place myself in the long gray line of scribblers who have done the same. Every one of us has something to say on the subject. It's what—we think—we do best. If you want to know how to make bacon, you might as well ask the pig.

Everyone will weigh in at some point along the spectrum that runs from mind-numbing, stress-inducing masochism, the waiting for the drop of blood on the forehead, to unalloyed ecstasy at the cashing of the paycheck or the discovery of "the best words in the best order," Coleridge's definition of poetry. Everyone will acknowledge the wisdom of Dr. Johnson's hardheaded professionalism and then go on to nod in agreement with Tennessee Williams, who, when asked why he wrote, replied simply, "Biological necessity." Any creative person will echo Williams: we can do no other. We have no choice. But we all feel at least some of the time that we are banging our heads against the metaphorical wall. One of the saddest, most instructive stories about writerly frustration was told by Colette of her father, a retired army captain who went to his study every day to compose his memoirs. No one in the family disturbed or interrupted him, and no one ever tried to open his pre-bound books, with printed titles like *My Campaigns*, *The Lessons of '70*, and *Marshal Mahon Seen by a Fellow Soldier*. When her father died, the family opened the books: they were all empty. He had not written a single word. How must he have spent his days? Sharpening his pencils? Looking out the window? Napping? All of us cringe. We know the terror of the blank page or, for most of us, the humming screen that cries out to be written upon. Are we desperately looking to fill that vacuum that Nature famously abhors?

Everyone needs stories; few people need writing. Taken all together, the great majority of the human race from the dawn of time has been illiterate. Socrates objected to writing, on the theory that once people can resort to reading they will lose the ability to remember, to think. You can question a person, but a book, if queried, will only say the same thing again. Generations have passed down their tales, songs, and poems orally, parent to child, village elders to novices, one generation to the next: this is how legend and myth perpetuate themselves.

Historians of reading and writing can tell us how these arts have developed—their technologies, methods, and purposes—but they seldom tell us about the deep joy that accompanies the creative act. Writers themselves–like those above–testify to the pains of their craft as the inevitable price and cause of its pleasures, of placing the best words in the best order, or of doing what the late Howard Nemerov said modestly of poetry: "A poem is getting something right in language."

Getting it right begins with getting it right with your hands. A writer is like a child playing with fingerpaints. These two messy manual activities often come to life simultaneously. Learning to write involves learning to shape the letters along straight lines as well as learning what to say and how to say it. People over a certain age can remember the Palmer method of handwriting, with its pattern of grids and lines within which we had to keep our perfectly shaped letters. We were taught to write by the book. Some of us can recall inkwells in wooden school desks, into which we dipped our steel-nibbed pens before applying ink to paper in maiden efforts that more often than not looked like Rorschach tests, all illegible blots and globs and spiderwebs.

When I was ten I wrote an entire newspaper. Reporter, writer, editor, designer, publisher, and proofreader, I was like a one-man band. Home from school with chicken pox or measles, in bed for much of a week but in no way incapacitated, I spent my time alternately dozing, reading, listening to the radio, and writing. I had propped a writing board, merely an extra wooden bookshelf, across the arms of a reading chair in my bedroom, and I sat with unlined paper, a ruler, and several colored pencils. With the ruler I made five vertical columns and some horizontal divisions. All the spaces–the whole plan looked like the start of a Mondrian painting–were meant to have articles, some of which would be self-contained, others of which would continue inside, as in the Philadelphia papers we saw every day, the *Inquirer* in the morning, the *Bulletin* in the afternoon. In the America of the 1950s, everyone read at least two daily papers, New Yorkers often more. I had the plan for the whole, I had the materials, and I had what journalists would call a page layout. What I didn't have was a subject. Like Colette's father, who presumably sharpened his pens and rearranged his beautifully bound books on his desk every day, I was ready to go. Until, that is, I had to start, at which point I stopped.

The choice of theme has always been the writer's first and most daunting task. The traditional writer of epic after Homer had to know what capacious story he was preparing himself to write. And the traditional epic poet wrote only a single epic, for which his entire life was the preparation. Virgil worked his way up to the *Aeneid*, Dante to the *Commedia*, Spenser to *The Faerie Queene* (unfinished at his death, as was the *Aeneid* at Virgil's), Camões to the *Lusiads*, and Milton to *Paradise Lost*. Whitman compiled *Leaves of Grass* over the course of his life, as did Ezra Pound his *Cantos*. The epic mode has come to include an accumulation of shorter poems, rather than a fully launched story, now that prose fiction has taken over from poetry the task of narration.

The writer must choose his topic, or hope that the Muse will come to him with a command and a subject. Thus, the Venerable Bede tells us of Caedmon, an illiterate seventh-century shepherd at Whitby Abbey, who was inspired to sing in a dream one night when visited by an angel. "What shall I sing?" he asked. "Sing to me of the Creation," the angel replied, which Caedmon dutifully did. Then, upon awakening, he went to the abbess and told her his dream. He recited the poem. Caedmon's "Hymn," all nine lines of it, is not only a song to Creation but also the start of English verse, an allegory of literary invention. Caedmon was inspired, and his story, like that of all the poets in the Western tradition from Homer to Pope, reminds us that sometimes things come to you that you could never have imagined. No one knows how or why. "What shall I sing?": that is the eternal question.

Some writers wait for the Muse. Some writers stick to a daily word limit. Anthony Trollope and Graham Greene are the most famous examples of strict self-discipline: they stopped when they reached the limit, even if in the middle of a sentence. Other people rely on other means, some on drugs and drink, the late American poet James

Merrill on voices revealed to him via the Ouija board, Yeats on the automatic handwriting of his wife, George. Some work best on assignment. The journalist's most helpful friend is the order: "I need three thousand words about this by tomorrow morning." The rest of us must look or reach around ourselves to find our sources.

But I digress, as Lord Byron once said of himself. After I had all my physical materials lined up, I had to begin my journalistic effort somehow. The physical form was at hand—something that resembled a newspaper—so why not, I asked myself, write some reports of things that actually happened? Local stories? Current events? News from the suburban home front? Backyard weather reports? My life and times? These might have sufficed, but they seemed so banal and insubstantial that I rejected them pretty quickly. Besides, because I was sick, I couldn't leave the house. I had been reading a children's series of biographies of our nation's first fathers and some other books of colonial American history, and then it came to me: I'll write a newspaper about the events leading up to and following July 4, 1776. After all, I am a Philadelphian and we saw the Liberty Bell and Independence Hall, Betsy Ross's house and Elfreth's Alley, on school trips. The lead article, on page 1, upper right, described the reading of Mr. Jefferson's Declaration. Others dealt with the city's weather during that stiflingly hot summer, and a profile of Dr. Franklin, Philadelphia's favorite non-native son, and his part behind the scenes. I'm sure that I invented certain shades of local color and created from whole cloth a cast of secondary characters, and I remember some especially inept illustrations done in colored pencil.

My newspaper, *The Philadelphia Ledger*, existed in a single copy; it ran for a single issue and was long ago deposited in the dustbin of history. It constituted not only a maiden speech but also a declaration of my own independence. From that time forth, I would write about things that had a reality of their own. I would embellish and interpret but not invent ex nihilo. I could have been a historian. Instead, I became a literary critic and a sometime journalist, basing my writing on something prior, and not unhappy to think of myself as secondary, responsive, or re-creative. Without knowing him or his words, I had thrown in my lot with the nineteenth-century Prussian Leopold von Ranke and his commitment to write history and *"zu zeigen, wie es eigentlich gewesen ist,"* to show how it actually was.

Some writers are cavalier, writing not only whenever the spirit moves them but also on matchboxes, napkins, whatever comes to hand. They are as unconcerned with their instruments as with the where and the how of writing. Others are obsessive about their location and materials, the physical implements of the trade. There are famous scenes of writing just as there are scenes of reading. Proust remained in his cork-lined room, blocking out all noise as well as noxious air. I knew a distinguished music writer who took his garage, which gave out onto an idyllic backyard, and converted it into his writing and listening studio. The first thing he did was to board up all the windows: he wanted no access to nature whatsoever, no distraction from his thoughts and the chores at hand. Edna Ferber was of the same mind: "The ideal view for daily writing, hour on hour, is the blank wall of a cold-storage warehouse. Failing this, a stretch of sky will do, cloudless if possible."

Like Proust, Edith Wharton wrote in bed, but for reasons other than health. She could stay uncorseted there, allowing herself various kinds of freedom not permitted to a proper lady. Writing by hand, tossing pages to the foot of the bed or on the floor, where they would be picked up and transcribed by her secretary, Mrs. Wharton led a writing life that every day preceded the other schedule that she followed once upright and dressed, ready to meet the world. Confined at the end of her life to her apartment bedroom in the Palais Royal in Paris, Colette wrote on a bed-raft, a *radeau-lit*, a table specially designed to fit over the bed. Throughout the twentieth century, writers became attached to their typewriters, to certain makes and ribbons and sounds. Henry James was so inspired by the actual clickety-clack of the keys as he dictated that often he required his secretary to begin typing before he had anything to say. Like one of Pavlov's dogs, James began to salivate after he heard the bell ring. Addiction, dictation, diction: they all come from the same root.

Some people stay at home, others leave it. The prolific John McPhee goes to an office near his house in Princeton and locks himself in for the day. When asked by an interviewer whether he receives pleasure from his writing, in addition to pain and frustration, he replied, "For about two minutes a day." As a young writer without much money, John Cheever rented a small studio in his Manhattan apartment building. Every morning he put on a suit and a tie, took the elevator down several floors, went into the office, and removed his suit and tie. He sat and wrote in his underwear until the end of the day, when he dressed and returned home. He was a commuting writer, as if getting ready for the suburban way of life he later chronicled.

Some writers have other specific rituals, mantras, or special needs. Others can work anywhere; Byron jauntily observed that he could compose on horseback or in the bath. The scattershot method sometimes produced nothing, but when he hit, or so he said, it was the real thing. He was one of the fast writers, along with Jack Kerouac and Allen Ginsberg, both of whom feigned a Byronic spontaneity, although both of them actually revised. Then there are the famously slow ones. Oscar Wilde: "I was working on the proof of one of my poems all the morning and took out a comma. In the afternoon I put it back again."

Most good writers work somewhere in between the two extremes, their words gushing out some of the time, at other times stumbling. Keats's famous dictum "If poetry comes not as naturally as leaves to a tree, it had better not come at all" represented only one side of the sedulous craftsman who revised painstakingly during his short writing life. "Ode to a Nightingale" was reputedly written in one morning. "On First Looking into Chapman's Homer," Keats's first great poem, came to him as he walked home to London after sharing an evening of poetry with his friend Charles Cowden Clarke, who received Keats's sonnet on his desk with the delivery of the morning post. But Keats also had plenty of trouble with other works, especially the longer ones, which he began, revised, and abandoned, not knowing how they would turn out. Most writers like to fuss, to *potchkie*, as one says in Yiddish. Thus, Yeats: "A line will take us hours maybe; / Yet if it does not seem a moment's thought, / Our stitching and unstitching has been nought." The appearance of spontaneity is a hard-won effort.

Some efforts go on forever. Wordsworth finished his *Prelude* in 1805 and, leaving it unpublished, worked on it for the remaining decades of his life, so that when it came out posthumously in 1850 it represented only partially the ideas and words of the younger man who was closer in age to the events in his past he was trying to reproduce. The original 1805 version appeared only in the twentieth century. Which is the real, or the better, *Prelude?* That is a question for every reader to answer for himself, with the use of a double text reproducing the two versions on facing pages. This is not a parlor game for the faint of heart.

Whatever else writing involves, and whatever differences exist among the scribbling tribe, most writers would agree with Orhan Pamuk that the writer's essential tool is "a commitment to being alone in a room." Although "Do you write with a pen? On a computer?" vies with "Where do you get your ideas?" as the most frequently asked question of writers, these things matter less than the sheer loneliness of the enterprise. Like everything else in this book but dancing, writing is a solitary act and brings solitary pleasure. If it causes pain, it also reminds us of the occasional bliss of solitude. Writing demands *Sitzfleisch*, the capacity to sit still, not squirm, and to begin, or to wait until beginning seems feasible. Some listen for the Muse; others agree with George Balanchine, who, when asked about inspiration, replied, "My muse must come to me on union time." The great choreographer knew that the clock was ticking, and that he needed to do his inventing between 10 and 1, between 3 and 6. A writer doesn't deal with unions, but he can still hear, at his back, Time's wingèd chariot hurrying near. Most writers are professionals. Some—the Flauberts,

Wildes, and E. A. Robinsons—revise so interminably that they cannot get to sentence two until sentence one is perfect. Others spew forth, then return to hack and chop, eliminate, reshape. Writing, as we all tell our students, is rewriting: it's always easier when you have something material in front of you to work with. Revision is another word for patience. Horace urged poets to put their stuff away for nine years and then take it out and have a second look. Can anyone today wait that long? Certainly not, if you read what passes for commentary on most blogs, which is for the most part unexamined and unrevised cries into the void of cyberspace.

The best method is to begin with a Big Bang, an explosion of thoughtless energy, and then gradually to take it all back in and shape it. At the start of his prose poem "The New Spirit," John Ashbery articulates every writer's dilemma: "I thought I could put it all down, that would be one way. And next the thought came to me that to leave it all out would be another, and truer, way." We can reimagine Ashbery's image in many metaphorical ways: exhalation and inhalation, expansion and contraction, expulsion and absorption. In her heartbreaking "North Haven," a memorial poem to her friend Robert Lowell, Elizabeth Bishop considers the differences between nature's cycles, the linearity of human life, and the artist's way of bridging the gap between the two: "Nature repeats herself, or almost does: / repeat, repeat, repeat; revise, revise, revise." Once dead, Lowell will no longer revise or change; like the maker himself, the work is finished. Bishop could not have predicted the way Lowell's editors or her own would begin the revisionary process after the poets' deaths, ransacking libraries, archives, and letters for early drafts, unfinished manuscripts, bits and scraps of paper, for evidence of a creative process that the poets themselves might not have wished to be made public.

Every writer with even a modest degree of self-consciousness can feel what Harold Bloom has labeled the anxiety of influence, the sense that the great masters, dead as well as living, are breathing down one's neck, inspiring and inhibiting in equal measure. The theory has the ring of truth even if you don't subscribe to the Freudian and Oedipal model on which Bloom bases it, namely that "strong" writers are compelled to castrate, murder, or otherwise symbolically destroy the father figure. The "ephebe," or youth, must absorb, reshape, and revise his predecessor's work, so that he can clear a space for himself. The young buck must kill the old one. Like nature, writers can be competitive, red in tooth and claw, whether the stakes are real or imagined, practical or merely metaphorical. W. J. Bate called the feeling—less threateningly—"the burden of the past." The envy of one's peers looms large; no writer is entirely without competitiveness. "It is not enough to succeed; others must fail," said La Rochefoucauld, articulating a basic human truth that few people, and still fewer artists, can ever evade.

But there are wiser, more modest voices. The late American poet William Stafford, a writer celebrated for speed and abundance, once met with a student who complained of writer's block; she couldn't get the words out correctly, nor could she be satisfied with something that wasn't absolutely right. Stafford's sage advice: "Lower your standards." Nothing ventured, nothing won. But then I think of Keats again: "I should rather fail than not be among the great." One has high ambitions. To honor them, one must enter the fray, although immortality will be determined only after we are all dead.

For whom does the writer write? His contemporaries? An imaginary audience? Does he wish to be a popular artist and to make money? That's one kind of success, although not a portent of immortality. Is he writing for the ages, as Bloom would suggest, for the Noble Dead, the great giants on whose shoulders he stands, and for the approval of the Old Masters? Everyone will weigh in with different answers to this question, even different answers at different times of the day. Writers are seldom contented with writing for themselves alone. As a form of communication, writing requires a communicator, an object to be communicated, and, at last, an audience for that object. Whom do you dream of when you write? To whom are you speaking? Who is your "you"?

As a literary editor who accepts invitations to conferences in order to address students, I am used to hearing the anxieties and the concerns of beginners of all ages. Only recently have I understood the one thing that separates writing from other forms of artistic endeavor and expression: namely, the desire, the strongly felt obligation, to be published. We should try to promote, instead, the phenomenon of "the Sunday poet," the writing version of the Sunday painter who takes her easel out on a weekend afternoon, does her drawings, sketches, watercolors, or oils, is grateful for the pleasure she has given herself, and then comes home. Or the piano player who tickles the ivories for his own benefit, singing along with himself to lower his blood pressure. Or the dancers who take to the floor at whatever venue—mosh pit, country club, Western dance hall, tango milonga—for the joys of dancing. The writer as amateur? Why not? Edna Ferber had some nasty things to say about this: "Only amateurs say that they write for their own amusement. Writing is not an amusing occupation. It is a combination of ditch-digging, mountain-climbing, treadmill and childbirth." But Ferber was both, like Dr. Johnson, a thorough professional and, like Tennessee Williams, a person compelled to do what she did. She needed to publish.

Publication—throwing oneself into an open sphere—is a relatively recent phenomenon, going back no more than three hundred years. Pope was the first great writer to take out a subscription; he asked people to support his translations from Homer with pre-publication sales and donations. Commercial publication began in earnest in the eighteenth century, and the world has not been the same since. The recent proliferation of self-published works, often by means of the Internet, is an expansion of as well as a throwback to the older tradition of distributing poems and other manuscripts among a circle of friends. Those circles are now virtually infinite. Your "friends" on MySpace may include people who really neither know you nor ever read a word you send out into cyberspace.

James Merrill once said that just thinking of the price exacted of becoming or wanting to become a popular writer turned him away from the chase for success—although success found him. At the end of his epic poem *The Changing Light at Sandover* Merrill imagines himself standing up to read everything he has just composed (more than six hundred pages) before an audience of his friends and family, the noble living and the noble dead, people from life, and others whom he has invented or invoked via the Ouija board throughout his epic. His poem ends by returning to its opening lines: "Admittedly, I err." Merrill is paying homage to his own master, W. H. Auden, who in his didactic poem *New Year Letter*, written in 1940 after he'd just arrived in the States from England, arranges a performance before a "tribunal" of his masters. Judgment and fame, laurels and immortality: the writer stands ready, waiting for them.

Writing for one's betters means taking long views and thinking of history's dark corridors. It also encourages the highest standards. About Auden the story is well known. When he went up to Oxford, he was assigned as his tutor at Christ Church the medieval scholar Neville Coghill. At their first meeting the world-wise don asked the student about his plans. I want to read English because I intend to be a poet, young Wystan said. Coghills's "Yes, of course, dear boy," or its equivalent, drew a longer, more assertive response: Mr. Coghill, you don't seem to understand. I am going to be a great poet. Coghill took notice. Ambition in the young is not a sufficient but it is certainly a necessary condition of greatness: Keats had it, as did Robert Lowell, the young T. S. Eliot, even the reticent Elizabeth Bishop, who knew before the rest of the world that she had the goods. And when you have the goods, you know you are writing for the ages, not for the immediate public.

Auden himself thought that the reason most people want to write has less to do with art or writing itself than with the artist's life and methods, with the fact that artists are their own masters. Only the lucky few actually are, but to the rest of the world, the artist's life looks more wonderful and enticing than the grind of a daily commute and watching the clock. Auden: "The idea of being one's own master appeals to most human beings, and this is apt to lead to the fantastic hope that the capacity for artistic creation is universal, something nearly all human beings, by virtue not of some special talent, but of their humanity, could do, if they tried." Lots of them keep trying, undaunted by rejection letters and a limited audience of friends and family. Like parents, teachers routinely encourage the young to "express themselves," and no one would deny the importance of the arts to a full education. None of the arts, however, makes you a better person, and nothing should promote the belief that anyone else has an interest in another person's pictures, songs, or poems, just as no one is interested in other people's travel photos, dogs, or children. One engages in the activity to please oneself, and if others want to overhear or to read it, so much the better. Playing an instrument makes you a better listener of good music; painting helps you to appreciate the Old Masters; and writing should lead you to be a better reader. That's the most you should count on.

As many have remarked, writers seem to outnumber readers. This observation has its own history. In 1783 Dr. Johnson said: "It is strange that there should be so little reading in the world, and so much writing. People in general do not willingly read, if they can have any thing else to amuse them." Writing certainly amuses them. Creative writing courses, degrees, and whole programs are now flourishing. They often provide colleges with something of a cash cow. Everyone can become a novelist or poet. Writers' conferences, full of the competent, the hopeful, and the deceived, in equal measure, allow people to sit at the feet of the master, to have the master read and comment upon their work, even if they have little interest in reading the work of the master him- or herself. Still, for at least two hundred years, everyone has complained about the proliferation of banal writing. The Hydra puts out more heads, do what we may to chop them off. Only history will sift through the accumulating pile of manuscripts and make judgments. Consider Melville, dying in obscurity with *Billy Budd* as yet unpublished, or Emily Dickinson and Gerard Manley Hopkins, whose poetic lives are entirely posthumous, or F. Scott Fitzgerald: *The Great Gatsby* garnered good reviews from the critics, but it failed to sell out its first printing.

Meanwhile, writers hold out hope for recognition and money, and the few to whom both come, those who win prizes and critical acclaim and can also support themselves through royalty checks, usually incite envy rather than gratitude from their rivals. Writers are contentious and envious of the successes of others, perhaps even more than painters, who require only a couple of gallery dealers or patrons to write checks for them. Shirley Hazzard said that "creative writing, alone among the arts, seems delusively accessible to every articulate person [and] has immemorially attracted that confusion of esteem and envy, centred on the independence in which it is conceived and composed." And thinking of her friend Graham Greene, who sold lots of books, Hazzard refers to the indignation of critics and aesthetes who rebuked the writer who had inspired millions of readers to buy his books and who, "having profited from that seemingly harmless transaction . . . had relinquished his immortal soul." Damned if you win the game, and ignored if you don't.

Writers—until they get too big for their metaphorical britches—enjoy fan mail, and often they graciously answer it. When my ten-year-old twin nieces told me they loved the preteen novels of Delia Ephron, I suggested they write her a letter, addressing it to her publisher. Timid and skeptical at first, they complied, and were delighted to get a thank-you note from their favorite author. I walked into a classroom one day and told my university students that I'd just finished a marvelous first book of poems by someone whom I didn't know, and immediately wrote her a letter. "You must always write fan letters, especially to poets, because they have no chance of making money, and more important, they have no idea whether anyone in the world is reading and responding to their work. Your letter will be like a lifeline." They nodded halfheartedly. A week later I returned with a note from the poet herself: "Dear Willard Spiegelman," it began. "Thank you so much for your kind words, for which I am deeply grateful. As you can imagine, we poets have no idea whether anyone is reading and responding to our work. Your letter was a lifeline. It reminded me that someone has. Yours sincerely, etc." Vindicated, I showed the note to my students.

Like virtue, writing must ultimately be its own reward. For the doing, one needs very little by way of material goods: a computer or just an old-fashioned pen and paper. Even libraries are less important than they are cracked up to be, and not only owing to an open, easier, universal access to knowledge via the Internet. The emigré scholar Erich Auerbach wrote *Mimesis*, one of the towering works of twentieth-century literary criticism, in Istanbul, where he sought refuge from the Nazis without any of his scholarly books. Relying only on primary texts (Homer, the Bible, et al.) and his intelligence and imagination, he composed a masterpiece. Necessity is the mother of many things. Deprivation can be inspiration. Graham Greene wrote a little book about the English dramatists on board ship in a wartime convoy, without books or even light to write by. A writer must only sit down and begin.

Sometimes exercises help. Like playing scales or noodling improvisations at the keyboard, drawing a perspective, shooting baskets in a playground, starting a yoga session with deep breathing, or rehearsing the one-two-three rise-and-fall of the waltz step, a writer starts afresh each time. Playing with language, as I said at the start, is like playing with fingerpaint. You mess around in it and see what you come up with, and that often takes on a life of its own, as the characters or words or thoughts veer off in a direction their maker may never have anticipated. Every writer has some version of the idea that the characters ran away with the story, or a poem that started as a sonnet decided it wanted to be something else. Scott Fitzgerald was never entirely satisfied with Jay Gatsby. He said, "I never at any one time saw him clear myself—for he started as one man I knew and then changed into myself." The mind has a mind of its own that we can't necessarily control. So does the inchoate beginning of a work of art, which flies from us just as we are trying to rope it in and shape it. It may have other ideas and intentions. Writing means striking a balance between your own will and the accidents that befall.

James Merrill's early poem "The Doodler" provides a charming glimpse into any artist's unconscious life. Addressing himself to the little random shapes he makes while talking distractedly to friends on the telephone, Merrill remarks on what he does and doesn't, can and cannot do, in part out of choice or talent, in part out of compensation for failures in his own life:

Noses as yet, alas, revert to profile.
Lips, too, are pursed in this or that direction,
Or raised to other lips from sheer distraction;
To mine not once. While still, just as at Deauville

Off-season, tiny hands are better hidden
By great muffs of albino porcupine.
Indeed, nothing I do is at all fine
Save certain abstract forms. These come unbidden:

Stars, oblongs linked, or a baroque motif
Expressed so forcibly that it indents
A blank horizon generations hence
With signs and pressures, massing to relief

Like thunderheads one day . . .

What are these images if not a metaphor for the creative act, with doodles standing in for the poems of the still self-deprecating young poet? Merrill's offhanded lyric seemingly celebrates the ease of doodling, the equivalent of automatic handwriting.

The fifteen drafts of the poem, however, show the pains he took to hammer his casualness into final shape. One must work to achieve apparent ease. Dr. Johnson: "What is written without effort is read without pleasure." Or: "Easy to read" means "hard to write." Easy writing usually makes for unprofitable reading. Examining drafts and revisions is the surest way to prove the ardors and also the mysteries of the writer's craft. Now that virtually everyone composes at the keyboard, we are in danger of losing the footprints of the creative act, although many savvy writers now use the "Track Changes" function in order to preserve the evidence of their creativity for a posterity they hope will be interested in it.

None of this, however, explains why any writers continue to do what they do. I think, again, of Auden, who, when approached by young people telling him they wished to become writers, asked why. If they responded "I want to express myself," he shook his head knowingly, sadly. If, instead, they said something like "Oh, I like to mess around with words; I like Scrabble and crossword puzzles; I like anagrams," he would smile and give them his avuncular blessing. We are all still children in the playroom with our fingerpaints, although in this case our fingers are working, more hygienically, with language. Edgar Degas said to his friend Stephane Mallarmé that he wanted to write poems because he had so many ideas banging around in his head. To which the wise Mallarmé replied, "A poem, my dear Degas, is written not with great ideas but with words."

Once upon a time I wrote a poem (see chapter 3). It began with a lightning flash of inspiration: looking at a painting reminded me of a line from Shakespeare. That was easy. I looked harder at the picture, trying to figure it out. More words came, and they came in iambic pentameter. John Hollander once said that free verse is easy to write if you don't know how. Blank verse—the standard rhythm of Shakespeare and Milton—is also easy, but for a different reason: it is embedded deep in the musical ear of anyone who has read and absorbed quantities of English poetry of the past six centuries. Shaw used to pooh-pooh Shakespeare's pentameter, perversely saying that any moron could improvise in blank verse, and then going on to do so himself. For Shaw, it was Shakespeare's prose passages, not the poetic ones, which testified to his genius. I discovered that once I had the rhythm down pat ("da-Dum, da-Dum, da-Dum, da-Dum, da-Dum") I began to think in verse. What came out was far from perfect, and it certainly required further attention, but initially the pattern allowed me freedom rather than confinement.

And once upon another time I wrote a short story. As with my maiden poem, everything came out of an opening line—"It was the names they had"—that occurred to me as I gazed out over a wintry New England landscape from a cold office on a gray February day and thought of my aunts and uncles, my parents' cousins, the generation born between 1912 and 1930. The story that followed—a bizarre effort in a style not my own—was brief, experimental, distinctly without a narrative base, and somewhat dreamy. It was really not a story at all, just a series of reconstructed scenes from childhood revised into a vague backward glance that in fact cast no light on anything important. A harmless effort, it went out into the world and was accepted by a literary quarterly. The acceptance letter arrived as I was standing by the faculty mailboxes, chatting with a student. "What is that?" he asked. "My first short story has just been accepted," I said. "Great. Are you going to write another one?" "No, I don't think so. I think one is more than enough." I had to prove, I suppose, something to myself by writing a story, but my heart wasn't in it. Why write fiction when reality has so much to offer? As with my early newspaper accounts of the American Revolution, composed in bed under semi-invalid conditions, I have preferred to focus my eyes on the world around me.

Why do I write? For one thing, it's something I can do with relative effortlessness. Facility counts for a lot. The sanguine person often takes the path of least resistance. Why do something that goes against a natural grain, that makes you sweat, that causes pain? Isn't it natural to look for pleasure through ease? Yeats wrote about "the fascination of what's difficult," and everyone not entirely indolent likes a good challenge now and again—but not too much of one. When she was a young woman, the fiction writer Jean Stafford worked one summer at a dude ranch in Colorado. One of the cowhands asked her what she wanted to do when she got out of college and grew up. She said she was going to become a writer. "That's nice work, Jean," he replied. "You can do it in the shade."

Why else do I write? For money, focus, and pleasure. (Why do I dance? Certainly not for money.) For more than two decades I have written occasional journalistic pieces for the Leisure & Arts page of *The Wall Street Journal*. Some years back my father asked me, "When did you become an expert on Renaissance terra-cotta sculpture?" To which I quickly replied, "When *The Wall Street Journal* offered me money to become one." What use, I say to my students, is a handful of fancy liberal arts degrees if you can't make yourself an expert on practically anything with a couple hours of work and by keeping your eyes and ears and mind open? In an age of increasing pre-professional education, the old-fashioned arts of reading and writing that have no immediate practical purpose have a great deal to recommend them. Give us more uselessness and we shall make of ourselves better adults. As dilettantes we shall discover usefulness ex post facto.

On the other hand, any university professor who writes literary scholarship can testify to the downside of impracticality, when reaching a limited or even a nonexistent audience and not getting paid to do so. At best, his audience is small; his payment, such as it is, even smaller. One does this both for the love of it and because one's employers demand it. Many years ago, the IRS summoned me to come into the office for an audit of my tax returns. Before my morning meeting I had spent a sleepless night envisioning stern officers who would clamp me in irons in the office and send me off to join people like Leona Helmsley in jail. "Found out at last," I said to myself, already imagining my farewells before heading to the slammer. For my interrogation, I figured that tweedy academic garb would suit me best, so I arrived looking like the Professor from Central Casting, which in fact is what I am. I sat cooling my heels in the antechamber, sweating and hyperventilating. I felt like a schoolchild who has been called to the principal's office.

Once beckoned into a small bureaucratic cell, I had an instructive interchange with the humorless but polite gorgon who was taking a look at my haphazard records, my shoebox full of meager receipts for "business-related" expenses. She was just doing her job, trying to collect the necessary facts. I was strictly small potatoes, and I knew that nothing the government could get out of me would have any impact on the national deficit. Still, I worried. A university press had just published my first scholarly book. "You claim these trips and other expenses as related to your book production," the woman observed, scanning the shreds of my papers and looking at me skeptically over the top of her half-glasses, "but I don't see any advance for the book."

"University presses don't give advances," I replied.

"And you don't claim any royalties," she helpfully observed.

"I won't earn any royalties on this. It has a limited run, and only university libraries will buy it."

"You mean you've written a book with no advance payment and no chance for royalties? You say this is a business, but there's no money that changes hands?"

She had never seen, or heard of, such a thing. Who, I wondered, was the naïve person in this exchange? I had written a book for the several hundred specialists throughout the world who would have an interest in my subject. I did it for pleasure, for truth and beauty, not money. My university patted me on the back. No one paid me, although I suppose that my proud dean increased my annual raise by a tenth of a percentage point or so. I had written about what I knew. Years of academic study had prepared me for this. Don Marquis once observed that writing a book of poetry and waiting for the reviews is like throwing rose petals into the Grand Canyon and then listening for the echo. It's a sad truth that applies to virtually all of us.

Luckily for me, the IRS inquisitor let me go free that October morning. I left the building with a weight lifted from my shoulders, and also with the old existential question ringing in my ears: Why are you doing this?

For a writer, working on something you *don't* know too much about has the advantage of not burdening you with the perils of expertise. This is the writer's equivalent of a teacher's decision to teach a new course to students rather than go over materials he may have been thinking about for decades. There's pleasure to be gained by starting in darkness and working your way up to some degree of light, rather than shining a high-beam lantern on a subject and obliterating the object as well as blinding the audience. Sanguine people like to learn—and try—new things. And doing new things adds to one's ratio of sanguinity.

Money is of course a great inducement to do anything. But so is the challenge—not only the ease—of focusing the mind. As with the requirement to write in iambic pentameter, so also with the defining limits of journalism. If my editor says he wants one thousand words, one thousand words is what I must deliver. There is modest wiggle room, but not much. Dr. Johnson said that "the prospect of hanging concentrates the mind wonderfully," and so does an editorial command. From constraint and constriction come inspiration and liberty. I had better know exactly what I wish to write about my subject, and I had better know which adjectives are dispensable, which necessary.

Repetition—also known as habit—is another incentive. I think of Cézanne returning to the same view of Mont Sainte-Victoire, of Giorgio Morandi and his bottles, of the photographer Ruth Orkin and the view from her balcony overlooking Central Park. Every venture, said Eliot, is a new beginning, "a raid on the inarticulate," even or especially when forging ahead into territory that looks the same but of course is not. Every day is a new day, every walk over the same terrain a new walk.

Every activity I have discussed in this book requires time, focus, and practice. Yet all of them encourage a degree of unconsciousness as well. You can listen to music and daydream, and then fall asleep. You can wander about in a daze, not noticing what you are seeing, and then walk into a tree. Hearing is not identical to listening, nor is seeing to looking. You can read a dense passage of Melville, Proust, or Faulkner, and realize, at the end of a chapter or even a page, that you don't remember what you've just read. But when writing, even when doodling with words, free-associating and (as they now say in the education business) brainstorming, you write down random thoughts, and then you return to them, those inchoate gestures, nouns without adjectives or verbs without subjects, and you begin to draw lines, fill in blanks, make connections. You see patterns, and as you see them, they change under your watchful eye and sedulous fingers. "How can I know what I think until I see what I say?": Forster's 1926 rhetorical question was picked up and quoted by Auden, among others, and has been so widely disseminated that many people think that they must have said it first themselves. Thinking precedes writing, but it also accompanies it. And then, in the process of revision—composed of equal parts of pain and excitement—it succeeds it. You work until you give in or you give up, and then you stop. Paul Valéry correctly observed that a poem is never finished; it is merely abandoned. Here, the painter has the advantage over the writer: at a certain point he says "Enough" and calls an end to it, applying his signature and then the vernissage. *Fini.* Quitting time. But writing can go on forever, like *Leaves of Grass*, never finished until its author himself was.

Any writer knows many kinds of frustrations. The kind that comes from personal dissatisfaction, the hour or day badly spent with nothing to show for it. The kind that comes from wondering whether anyone will care about, indeed even read, what you have written. The kind that comes from envy, pure and simple, of the successes of others whom you consider your inferiors or equals, and the more debilitating envy that comes from the heroic achievements of your betters. Graham Greene said, upon reading *War and Peace*: "What's the use of ever writing again—since this has been done. The book was like some great tree, always in movement, always renewing itself." In her handbook *Reading Like a Writer* Francine Prose begins with her version of a twelve-step AA self-help program. She admonishes us and says we must first acknowledge the existence of a higher being, Shakespeare, for example. Then we write.

And then comes pleasure, after the disappointments, false starts, and wrong turns, beginnings with no endings, superfluities, endings that do not give the satisfaction of genuine closure. Maybe two minutes a day. Perhaps more. These minutes compensate for the mismanaged hours and the pages left on the cutting-room floor, the drafts discarded, the beginnings obliterated. By definition creative work is not efficient. We must accept our false starts and our full wastebaskets as the conditions for our modest successes. Writers are children in the sandbox. We move things around, we make messes and then clean them up. We add, then we subtract. We circulate, as if heeding Stevens's adage that merely going round is good. We spin our wheels. And then we stop.

The aftermath of the pain of writing often involves a self-acknowledgment of, and an alertness to, the forms in which one has worked. Every so often one feels "the achieve of, the mastery of the thing" (Hopkins), the thrill of "getting something right in language" (Nemerov), of discovering a momentary mathematical accuracy, an astonishing verbal combination. The writer's satisfaction comes not from without but from within. Writing about dancing, I applied both T. S. Eliot's "You are the music while the music lasts" and Willa Cather's epitaph about happiness: "to be absorbed into something complete and great." Writing about writing, I'll apply them again. You commit yourself in total concentration, but you also give yourself up in the process. In so doing, you find yourself, even though you are not sure who that person is. Fitzgerald said that all good writing is "swimming underwater and holding your breath." The currents are swift and you may, when submitting yourself to the destructive element, endanger your own safety. But then you come up for air. You have seen the depths. You are ready to start again.

Francis Bacon observed with epigrammatic precision in his essay "On Studies": "Reading maketh a full man, conference a ready man, and writing an exact man." I have tried to take this lesson to heart and to make it the cornerstone of my life as a teacher. I quote it whenever I'm confronted by the highfalutin theorists and educational experts in the Groves of Academe. What goes on in the classroom? First we read some things, then we talk about them, and then we write about them. Reading fills us, discussion prepares us, and writing, the fruits of our labors, exacts from us a certain toil and then makes us–think of the proper synonyms for "exact"–precise, faithful, meticulous, organized, thorough.

That's right, exactly right. Or close, at least metaphorically right. For the sanguine person, "close" is often good enough.

Acknowledgments

I am grateful to Martha Kaplan, high school chum from long ago and literary agent of today, for getting this book into the world. At Farrar, Straus and Giroux, Jonathan Galassi saw enough in my proposal to give me the go-ahead; he has encouraged me at every step of the way. His assistants at FSG, Jesse Coleman and Zachary Woolfe, have helped immeasurably. I owe special thanks to Kenneth Bleeth and Laura Furman for their advice, counsel, and suggestions. Some years back, Jeanne Haflinger and Olivia Nicholas got me to dance; I guess they count as Terpsichorean muses.

This book opened with a description of its genesis, on the dance floor and in an airplane conversation. I have written the bulk of the actual pages in different places, at different times, under different conditions. What I think of as the "active" chapters—those about the body—began as magazine pieces and have been expanded for inclusion here. I am grateful to J. D. McClatchy, Mark Oppenheimer, and Robert Wilson for having published earlier versions of these essays, on dancing, walking, and swimming, in *The Yale Review*, *In Character*, and *The American Scholar*.

I pulled everything together in paradisal, or at least extremely comfortable, circumstances. I spent the month of September 2007 at the Villa of the Pines (Villa dei Pini), a part of the Bogliasco Foundation, five miles east of Genoa on the Ligurian coast. I worked in a studio above the Mediterranean, which I looked at from my windows and listened to as it hit the rocks beneath the pine forest that separated me from it. I spent a lot of time gazing and daydreaming. The sea's reassuringly steady sound invariably inspires an equivalent, subconscious rhythm in any working writer, painter, or composer. I lived there in the company of seven other fellows and their partners. We guests took meals together; we conversed in several languages; we enjoyed a daily cadence that swung between conviviality and privacy. I spent most of my day alone. The meals and the outings—some solo, some in company—punctuated the bliss of solitude indoors.

Talking it over with Karl and Kay Stead, the two wisest guests at Bogliasco, I realized a crucial truth about Paradise: although we know we must leave it eventually, there is no reason to do so before we have to. Why hasten, rather than postpone, the expulsion? I told the Steads that I felt only the most modest twinge of hesitancy, or of guilt, at not wanting to explore the coast, to visit yet another picturesque Riviera village, to climb another hill, or to watch the boats in the harbor at Portofino. I had done these things when I was younger. This couple is worldly, well-traveled, and clever. They agreed with me. Should we play hooky and go to a much touted local restaurant? Why? It's only a meal. Should we hike the paths at Le Cinque Terre? No. The vegetation and terrain there resemble ours here, some miles to the west. Staying here suffices. Something different would not necessarily constitute something new. Dr. Johnson once admitted that a few things are worth seeing, but remained convinced that nothing is worth going to see. I could make the same one-hour *passeggiata al mare*, the stroll along the seawall between Bogliasco and Nervi, every day, assured that today's walk, like the sea we were listening to, looking at, and swimming in, was both the same as and different from yesterday's.

We all spent our time contentedly doing what we like best. We had no dancing in this group of academics and artists, I am sad to say, but each day I read, wrote, swam, walked, looked, and listened. My senses were alert, my brain and body both responsive and then active. I took things in, I thought about them, I wrote about them. The pace and schedule here allowed a real-life application of Bacon's wise epigram that I have quoted previously: "Reading maketh a full man, conference a ready man, and writing an exact man." This life of active leisure was possible largely because the banal requirements of real life—errands, cooking, cleaning, domestic and professional obligations—had been magically, albeit temporarily, removed. I had no commitments to anything beyond myself. Time, making no demands, had momentarily stopped. I must express my enormous gratitude to the Bogliasco Foundation and to its always helpful office staff: Anna Maria Quaiat, Ivana Folle, and Alessandra Natale.

This book—I think of it as my book of gerunds, à la Henry Green—has dealt with seven important activities that bring pleasure. Everyone can make his or her own list of pleasures, favorite things like whiskers on kittens, or objects, activities, and pastimes that raise a smile, lighten the heart, or lift the spirits. Bertolt Brecht, whom I doubt anyone would think of as the Oscar Hammerstein, Jr., of his day, compiled such an inventory of *Vergnügungen* (pleasures), which Lotte Lenya recorded in her inimitable gravelly *Sprechstimme*, that cross between speech and song. His catalogue of sixteen overlaps in part with mine: "the old book come across again," "showering, swimming," "old music," "writing, planting," "traveling," "singing."

I have omitted the one gerund of pleasure that exists implicitly throughout most of these pages. I might have paid more attention to it. In addition to reading, walking, looking, dancing, listening, swimming, and writing, the most elementary activity of the sanguine life is sitting. "All mankind's troubles are caused by one single thing, which is their inability to sit quietly in a room" (Pascal, *Pensées*, II, 139). That just about sums it up.